Sarah Mercer's and Herbert Puchta's 101 Psychological Tips

T0005966

Cambridge Handbooks for Language Teachers

This series, now with over 50 titles, offers practical ideas, techniques and activities for the teaching of English and other languages, providing inspiration for both teachers and trainers.

The Pocket Editions come in a handy, pocket-sized format and are crammed full of tips and ideas from experienced English language teaching professionals, to enrich your teaching practice.

Sarah Mercer's and Herbert Puchta's 101 Psychological Tips

Sarah Mercer and
Herbert Puchta

Consultant and editor: Scott Thornbury

Shaftesbury Road, Cambridge CB2 8EA, United Kingdom

One Liberty Plaza, 20th Floor, New York, NY 10006, USA

477 Williamstown Road, Port Melbourne, VIC 3207, Australia

314–321, 3rd Floor, Plot 3, Splendor Forum, Jasola District Centre, New Delhi – 110025, India

103 Penang Road, #05–06/07, Visioncrest Commercial, Singapore 238467

Cambridge University Press & Assessment is a department of the University of Cambridge.

We share the University's mission to contribute to society through the pursuit of education, learning and research at the highest international levels of excellence.

www.cambridge.org
Information on this title: www.cambridge.org/9781009343701

First published 2023

20 19 18 17 16 15 14 13 12 11 10 9 8 7 6 5 4 3 2 1

Printed in Great Britain by CPI Group (UK) Ltd, Croydon CR0 4YY

A catalogue record for this publication is available from the British Library

ISBN 978-1-009-34370-1 Paperback
ISBN 978-1-009-34369-5 eBook
ISBN 978-1-009-34368-8 Cambridge Core

Contents

The authors and publishers acknowledge the following sources of copyright material and are grateful for the permissions granted. While every effort has been made, it has not always been possible to identify the sources of all the material used, or to trace all copyright holders. If any omissions are brought to our notice, we will be happy to include the appropriate acknowledgements on reprinting and in the next update to the digital edition, as applicable.

Key: T = Tip

Text

T4: Oxford University Press for the adapted text from 'Positive Organization Development: Innovation-inspired Change in an Economy and Ecology of Strengths', by David L. Cooperrider and Lindsey N. Godwin, *The Oxford Handbook of Positive Organizational Scholarship* by Gretchen M. Spritzers, and Kim S. Cameron. Copyright © 2013 Oxford University Press. Reproduced with kind permission of Oxford University Press via PLSclear; **T35:** Taylor Francis Group for the adapted text from 'Clearly communicating the learning objective matters! Clearly communicating lesson objectives supports student learning and positive behavior' by Deborah K. Reed, *Middle School Journal*, Vol 43. Copyright © 2012 Taylor Francis Group. Reproduced with kind permission from Taylor and Francis Group via Copyright Clearance Center; **T62:** Springer Nature for the adapted text from 'Development and use of the ARCS model of instructional design' by John M. Keller, *Journal of Instructional Development*, Vol 10. Copyright © 1987 Springer Nature. Reproduced with kind permission from Springer Nature via CCC.

Typesetting

Typeset by QBS Learning.

Thanks

The authors would like to thank Alison, Jo and Karen for their support and encouragement.

Why we wrote this book

An understanding of psychology is fundamental to good teaching practice. All teachers need to understand the basics of psychology such as how to motivate learners, reduce anxiety, prompt engagement, develop positive group dynamics, etc. However, very often the advice in this area covers big issues such as 'build positive rapport with learners' or 'develop a sense of group identity'. These are important things to do, but they take time and are not amenable to easy interventions. For some, it may also be unclear where to begin in concrete terms with practical steps to turn these notions into action. There are no quick fixes for psychological issues and there is no one-size-fits-all approach to psychological interventions – every teacher, learner, group and educational context is different. Nevertheless, there are some specific actions which have been shown to generally lead to positive changes in thinking and behaviour.

In this book, we draw on research and theory from psychology to suggest practical tips to language teachers for small changes you can make to your practice which lead to positive effects on learning and/or teaching. The tips centre on three main areas of influence: language teachers' own psychology; that of your learners; or that of the group as a whole. In order to be included in the collection, a tip must fulfil two core criteria: (1) it must be a relatively small and easy intervention in concrete terms that teachers can make; and (2) there must be some evidence that this action can impact on learning/teaching behaviours and outcomes. In this way, the book is based largely on research and evidence, but remains extremely practical, grounded, and easy to implement. However, there is a caveat to add here. The outcomes of educational research can often be interpreted in different ways and there will always be diverse opinions about their practical application. Furthermore, a host of factors can influence the effect of any intervention depending on localised and individual factors. Indeed, given that language teaching is inextricably tied to social and cultural contexts, the interpretation and application of such research will vary and be locally determined. As such, we are aware others may hold different opinions, and every reader will need to critically reflect on the appropriacy of any tip for you and your learners in your specific cultural and institutional setting. Given that this book is designed to be short and easy to engage with, we have omitted lengthy discussions of issues surrounding the advice and instead we have adopted a stance based on our experiences, convictions and understanding of theory, literature and existing research. For simplicity, we have included only one or two references for each tip to illustrate the evidence and suggest pathways of further reading.

Naturally, we do not expect teachers to try to employ all 101 tips at once – that might even be counter-productive and create an express route to burnout. We offer this collection of psychological tips as a palette of ideas and actions to choose from, and each teacher will use your own experience and expertise to make decisions what to use, when, and maybe how to adapt.

We have organised the book around six core areas of the psychology of language learning and teaching. We begin, in section A, by suggesting a selection of tips for teacher wellbeing which is a crucial but often overlooked component of good practice. The emotional state of teachers can impact on the entire learning dynamics of individuals and the group. Next, we consider the ways in which a teacher can lead a group or class with compassion, authority and skill. This section encompasses aspects of methodology, classroom management techniques and interpersonal skills. The focus in section C is on the socio-emotional climate of the group as a whole and diverse aspects of group dynamics. The focus then switches to the learner as an individual and concentrates on three key psychological areas that are defining for language learning success: learner engagement, self-esteem and empowerment (also known as *agency*). The aim is to cover core psychological areas for the teacher, the learner and the class as a whole in ways that will positively impact on their psychological, socio-emotional and motivational states.

We expect the book to be relevant for teachers of all students, as many aspects covered are central to human learning and language processing at all levels and ages. The book and tips can be read in any order, but we do recommend you commence with the first section about your own psychology and wellbeing. It is perhaps the most important area to address before reflecting on what ways you can care for others. We hope the book inspires and supports you as language teachers.

A: Psychological tips for teacher wellbeing

Wellbeing refers to the sense of satisfaction, meaning and balance a person feels. It is more than just positive emotions; it involves experiencing manageable levels of stress and leading a life that feels personally satisfying. We start the book with a section on teacher wellbeing as we believe it is the foundation of good practice.

1 Be unapologetic about taking time for self-care
2 Set boundaries
3 Find a time management strategy that works for you
4 Focus on strengths
5 Be a good colleague
6 Learn when to exercise acceptance
7 Seek out the positives
8 Remind yourself of the meaning of your work
9 Gain different perspectives on unsuccessful lessons
10 Find a friend at work
11 Celebrate who you are as a teacher
12 Plan your own professional development
13 Plan time for hobbies and small treats
14 Know how to manage your emotions
15 Use proactive strategies in the classroom
16 Learn to satisfice
17 Tweak your job to make it more enjoyable
18 Connect with nature regularly
19 Take mindful minutes
20 Know the signs of burnout
21 Use a wellbeing checklist

1 Be unapologetic about taking time for self-care

> Taking time to engage in self-care is essential for wellbeing, so teachers can teach to the best of their abilities.

Our first tip is deliberately chosen to highlight how important it is for language teachers to attend to their wellbeing and take time for their own self-care. Self-care refers to consciously paying attention to your physical, emotional and mental wellbeing. To do so is not a selfish indulgence, but rather it is a basic necessity for healthy functioning.

Ideally, the responsibility for wellbeing lies not only with the teacher, but it is actively supported by the social context and institutions where educators work. However, this is not always the case. While self-care can never compensate for precarious and difficult work conditions, it remains one important strategy that teachers can engage in to protect and nurture their wellbeing.

Teacher wellbeing is fundamental for good practice as it helps educators to teach more creatively, build better relationships with others, and cope with daily stressors among other benefits. One challenge is that teachers tend to be very other-oriented: in their dedication to their jobs and families, they often spend all their time on meeting the needs of others. Yet, 'you cannot pour from an empty cup'. It is vital that teachers deliberately set aside time to engage in self-care by:

1. Understanding your needs and what kind of things nourish you, e.g., hobbies, nature, socialising, music, art, alone time, reading, yoga, spirituality, etc. (see **13** and **18**).
2. Keeping a log of your self-care activities to make visible your actions.
3. Attending to the health triangle: nutrition, sleep and exercise.
4. Marking out 'me time' in the calendar and committing to it.
5. Seeking out help or social support if feeling overwhelmed.
6. Engaging in any of the other tips in this section that appeal!

Mercer, S. & Gregersen, T. (2020). *Teacher Wellbeing*. Oxford: Oxford University Press.

Turner, K. & Thielking, M. (2019). Teacher wellbeing: Its effect on teaching practice and student learning. *Issues in Educational Research, 29*(3), 938–960.

Creating boundaries and being able to detach from work is important for wellbeing and life satisfaction.

The majority of teachers often take work home, and even engage in professional development outside working hours. The boundaries between work and home life become blurry: a situation exacerbated by the shift to online teaching. While some people may relish the flexibility of this work mode, others have difficulties creating boundaries and struggle to detach, which can negatively impact their wellbeing, life satisfaction and relationships.

The term *work/life balance* was intended to capture the notion of an integration of work and non-work. However, the term is misleading. Firstly, there is no such mythical state of perfect balance. It is constantly changing, and every person has different needs in this regard. Secondly, the words themselves create the impression we have two separate domains: work and life. We have life; one life, which must incorporate our work as well as our non-work lives.

To manage a healthy synthesis of work and non-work, it can help to create three types of boundaries:

1. *Temporal boundaries*: This refers to deliberately setting time aside for leisure, family and friends. Put time for self-care in one's calendar and protect that as a fixed appointment. Ensure evenings and weekends include sufficient non-work time.
2. *Spatial boundaries*: Working from home can mean there is no physical escape from work. Keep work restricted to one room, one set of bookshelves, or tidied away in your bag when you are not working. Home needs to be a place for relaxation and disconnection.
3. *Technological boundaries*: Switch off technology, and disable notifications. Ask yourself whether students and/or parents need your contact details outside of work.

Sonnentag, S. & Fritz, C. (2015). Recovery from job stress: The stressor-detachment model as an integrative framework. *Journal of Organizational Behavior, 36,* 72–103.

3 | Find a time management strategy that works for you

Time management strategies reduce stress and anxiety, by giving teachers a sense of control over their time.

Many teachers feel they have more things to do in a day than there are hours available. This means everyone needs to decide on their priorities and what they allocate their time to. *Time management* refers to strategies that you consciously employ in order to take control of how you use your time. Research shows that using time management strategies can help reduce anxiety and stress, acting as a buffer against burnout and exhaustion. It is important to understand that time management strategies must be utilised to ensure time for leisure, friends and family, not just work.

There are many time management strategies, but it is important to find the one that works for you as an individual. Here are some examples:

- *Time blocking*: This is when you set aside a realistically estimated block of time for a specific task and ensure it is completed within that time. Also build in buffer zones to reduce stress and leave space for the unexpected. Be sure to schedule leisure blocks, too.
- *Pomodoro technique*: A strategy which involves working intensively without any distractions for 20–25 minutes and then taking a five-minute break. After four such blocks of work, it is then recommended to take a longer break of around 30 minutes.
- *To-do list*: The most traditional strategy, which involves drawing up a list of what needs to be done short- and long-term as well as possibly setting priorities in degrees of urgency and deadlines (e.g., list A to be done today; list B this week; list C this semester).
- *Learn to say no*: Saying no to unnecessary or unenjoyable requests frees up time to say yes to other things you would rather do.

Misra, R. & McKean, M. (2000). College students academic stress and its relationship to their anxiety, time management, and leisure satisfaction. *American Journal of Health Studies*, 16(1), 41–51.

> **A strengths-based approach to education looks at identifying and building on strengths for growth.**

In education, there can be a tendency to focus on weaknesses and deficits in learners as well as teachers. Teachers are encouraged to reflect on what went wrong in their classes, what needs improving, and how to solve problems in their practice. While that can be useful, it also risks creating a sense of perpetual dissatisfaction and negativity. Professional improvement can also come from building on successes and strengths, not just from addressing weaknesses. Indeed, the use of 'can-do' statements in learning contexts is an attempt to foster a more positive sense of achieved competence.

One suggestion of how to focus on strengths is to use Appreciative Inquiry (AI) (Cooperrider & Godwin, 2013). AI encourages individuals or groups of people to identify and critically reflect on their successes and strengths, and consider how these can be built upon or transferred to other contexts. The authors propose a 4D cyclic model to carry out AI:

1. *Discovery*: What are my strengths and successes? Why was something successful? What contributes to my strengths?
2. *Dream*: How would I want my classes to look?
3. *Design*: How could I use my strengths or understanding of my successes to achieve this vision?
4. *Destiny*: What happens when I transfer my insights from my successes or strengths in other contexts?

Next time you reflect on your teaching or engage in peer observation, take an AI approach and learn from moments of success and strengths. What went well, why, and how can we use that knowledge in the future?

Bushe, G. R. & Kassam, A. F. (2005). When is appreciative inquiry transformational: A meta-case analysis. *Journal of Applied Behavioral Science, 41*(2), 161–181.

Cooperrider, D. L. & Godwin, L. N. (2013). Positive organizational development: Innovation-inspired change in an economy and ecology of strengths. In Cameron, K., & Spreitzer, G. M. (Eds.), *The Oxford Handbook of Positive Organizational Scholarship* (pp. 737–750). Oxford: Oxford University Press.

5 Be a good colleague

Being kind to others can have a positive influence on our own emotions and our physical and mental health.

In a meta-study on the effect of altruism on adults, Post (2005) shows that there are clear correlations between caring about and being kind to others and our own physical and mental health, emotions and even longevity. Supporting others 1) makes us feel more connected socially, 2) diverts us from our own problems, 3) gives meaning to our actions, 4) leads to an increased perception about our efficacy, and 5) contributes to a more active lifestyle. Moreover, it enhances our creativity, flexibility and openness to new ideas and new information.

However, we should aim at reasonable altruism, remaining aware that it's possible to get overwhelmed by attempts to care for others. It has also been shown that being caring in order to get rewards rather than genuinely being motivated by concern for others does not have the positive effects listed above.

Here are a few ideas of how to be a good colleague:

- If you notice a colleague is stressed or feeling down, show your empathy and offer your support by, e.g., sitting down for a cup of coffee with them and offering to listen to them actively if they want to share what's bothering them.
- You may engage in doing 'random acts of kindness' – e.g., offer to help a colleague carry out an unpleasant task; ask a colleague how their day is going; bring some treats for the coffee break for everyone to share; offer to become a mentor for a colleague in their first year of teaching; SMILE!
- Get engaged in volunteer work, e.g., become an active member of a teachers' association.

Post, S. G. (2005). Altruism, happiness, and health: It's good to be good. *International Journal of Behavioral Medicine, 12*(2), 66–77.

Learn when to exercise acceptance   6

> **Acceptance is a coping strategy which can lower stress levels and reduce the risk of burnout.**

When people have good or bad experiences, they explain the reasons for them as being either due to things within their control (*internal locus of control*, e.g., my use of strategies or effort) or to things outside their control (*external locus of control*, e.g., a colleague or luck). Those who have an internal locus of control are likely to feel that they can change things and make a positive difference. This sense of control, as opposed to feeling helpless, is empowering and can significantly reduce stress.

A related coping strategy is that of acceptance. Some things are truly out of our control. When appropriate, learning to accept those things means we can stop worrying about them and move on to expending our energy elsewhere. The key is to understand which things are within our control. Ruminating over something we cannot change is wasted time and emotion. However, there are also instances where acceptance is not appropriate. Accepting things we are unhappy about but could change will lead to dissatisfaction. For example, we may be facing unacceptable work conditions in which seeking change, support, or choosing to leave the situation may be the wiser path of action.

- Identify the problem you are concerned about.
- Brainstorm as many reasons as possible why this issue is as it is.
- Consider whether any of these reasons are within your control.
- Is the situation so unacceptable that you need to agitate for change or leave?
- Choose a path of action based on what you can control and what is reasonable for you to accept. Consider how you will feel one year from now about this decision.

Nakamura, Y. M. & Orth, U. (2005). Acceptance as a coping reaction: Adaptive or not? *Swiss Journal of Psychology*, 64(4), 281–292.

7 Seek out the positives

> To ensure emotional balance, it is important to consciously seek out the positives.

Humans have a natural negativity bias, which means we tend to focus more on the negatives of a situation. Through habit, we can train ourselves to look out for and identify positives. This does not mean ignoring the negatives in life or suppressing negative emotions. Rather, it is about ensuring we have emotional balance and can become aware of the positives around us (see **21**).

One strategy for seeking out the positives is to find 'silver linings' when we experience a stressful or difficult situation. This means looking at our experience and thinking consciously of those aspects which are positive, any possible benefits, or ways in which we were fortunate, as the situation could perhaps have been even worse.

Another strategy to boost positive emotions is to create a *positivity portfolio*. This is a folder in which you regularly collect the things that remind you of happy moments in your life. You could include a kind email from a colleague; photos of special moments, places or people; or a drawing from a student. When things are not going so well, you will have something to guide you back to feeling more positive.

Finally, another key source of positivity can be your own inner voice. Self-compassion is about being kind to yourself. It means treating yourself as you would your dearest friend. Teachers can often be their own fiercest critic, judging their mistakes harshly, calling out their own shortcomings, and comparing themselves negatively to others. Self-compassion encourages you to talk kindly to yourself, identify your strengths and successes, and accept that all humans are imperfect and make mistakes.

Cassidy, T., McLaughlin, M. & Giles, M. (2014). Benefit finding in response to general life stress: Measurement and correlates. *Health Psychology and Behavioral Medicine*, 2(1), 268–282.

Fredrickson, B. (2011). *Positivity: Groundbreaking research to release your inner optimist and thrive*. Oxford: Oneworld Publications.

Neff, K. (2011). *Self-compassion: The proven power of being kind to yourself*. New York: Harper Collins.

Remind yourself of the meaning of your work

Reminding yourself of the difference your work can make to others supports your motivation and wellbeing.

According to Nelson Mandela, 'Education is the most powerful weapon to change the world.' When asked why they initially wanted to become teachers, many frequently refer to higher goals, such as wanting to help students develop as human beings or contribute positively to society. For language teachers, they may be driven by the ability to empower students for global interaction and to contribute to intercultural understandings. However, given the stress teachers frequently suffer from, it is not surprising that many teachers can lose sight of their initial motivations and these meaningful dimensions to their work.

Schueller and Seligman (2010) mention pleasure, engagement and meaning as three pathways towards wellbeing. Pleasure, such as watching a great movie or eating a delicious dessert, can boost one's mood but does not contribute to wellbeing beyond that moment. Engagement and meaning, however, have been shown to be positively correlated with wellbeing in the long term. They promote positive relationships, help us set effective goals, and allow us to stay connected to our sense of purpose.

- Think about your initial motivation to become a teacher. Imagine a dialogue between yourself from that time and you now. Take notes of any insights it might give you.
- Notice when you feel more strongly connected to your sense of purpose. When are you most actively engaged?
- Chat with colleagues who seem very engaged. Ask them how they feel about their work and what drives them. Is there anything you can learn from them?
- Leave a note or image near your desk to remind yourself every day of why what you do matters to the world at large.

Schueller, S. M. & Seligman, M. E. P. (2010). Pursuit of pleasure, engagement, and meaning: Relationships to subjective and objective measures of well-being. *The Journal of Positive Psychology*, 5(4), 253–263.

Gain different perspectives on unsuccessful lessons

When a lesson has gone badly, the problem might be our perception of things, rather than what actually happened.

Thinking of a lesson that had gone badly, a colleague said: 'I planned this lesson really carefully and thought it was going well. But, in the last few minutes, I asked the students to give me feedback. One of them said she found it boring. I was so disappointed that I even thought of giving up teaching!'

What's striking is that this colleague felt the lesson went wrong – and even thought of giving up teaching – based on the feedback he got from just **one** student. When pressed about the feedback from other students, he said that it seemed to be OK, but could not really remember.

In a situation like that, the technique of cognitive reframing might be helpful. Here's an analogy: when we change the frame around a picture, chances are that our perception of the picture might change, too. That's what cognitive reframing does: it helps us find different perspectives on a problem so we can come up with more constructive interpretations.

Limiting thinking patterns are:

- Generalizations: *None of my students likes me*;
- Making a mountain out of a molehill (as in the anecdote above);
- Limiting beliefs: *I can't tell stories to a group of students. I'm too shy.*

Here are a few cognitive reframing techniques to try cognitive reframing:

- Ask yourself: *If a good friend of mine had experienced this, what advice would I give them?*
- With limiting beliefs (*I can't...*), ask yourself questions such as: *What would happen if I could? What stops me from being able to ...?*

Clark, D. A. (2013). Cognitive restructuring. In Hoffman, S. G., Dozois, D. J. A., Rief, W. & Smits, J. (Eds.), *The Wiley Handbook of Cognitive Behavioral Therapy* (pp. 1–22). Hoboken, NJ: John Wiley & Sons.

Being part of a social network is important for your wellbeing and helps you cope better with stress.

How we spend time at our workplace is key to our wellbeing in two ways: how much we like what we do, and the rapport we have with others around us. Research has shown that the amount of time we devote to building relationships matters, even short intervals of informal chatting increase our productivity and happiness at work (see 5). Interestingly, even small attempts at improving social cohesiveness significantly increase our wellbeing and willingness to engage.

Having a friend at work has been shown to improve wellbeing as it allows us to have a partner to share our ups and downs with and gives us a sense of not being alone through our shared experiences.

- Make sure you find topics of conversation beyond work. Find common interests, chat about the weekend, remember your colleague's partner's name, etc.
- Face-to-face communication is better than digital channels, but occasional kind messages on social media can put a smile on people's faces, too. Never underestimate the value of handwritten personal notes!
- Are you perhaps worried that others might not be interested in a friendship with you? Well, find out by simply giving it a try. You may well find that by breaking the ice, you'll have relieved your colleague of the worry of doing that themselves.
- Especially for new colleagues, reach out and suggest doing some team teaching together or offer to meet to exchange news and views.
- Why not join a teaching association as a great way to find colleagues and friends from beyond your own institution?

Rath, T. & Harter, J. (2010). Your friends and your social wellbeing. *Gallup Business Journal*. Retrieved on October 22, 2022, from: https://store.gallup.com/p/en-us/10410/wellbeing:-the-five-essential-elements.

11 Celebrate who you are as a teacher

> Your authenticity as a teacher contributes to your
> wellbeing and can impact positively on your students, too.

Studies have shown that while pre-service teachers frequently see the
process of becoming a teacher as a learning experience that includes
trial and error, once in the profession, they believe they need to enact
their vision of a successful teacher who has to be highly competent with
no room for error. 'If adopted, this belief can lead student teachers to
underprivilege their own authentic development and to overprivilege
surviving, impressing observers, or enacting teaching as an artificial
performance on the public stage of a classroom' (Olsen, 2016, pp. 32–33).

Becoming an authentic teacher is about learning who you want to
be as a teacher and acting in line with your self vision, as opposed to
performing a role in line with the perceived expectations of others. This
process may not always be easy and how you wish to be as a teacher
may change throughout your career. However, being authentic as a
teacher benefits your wellbeing and helps your learners to trust you.

- To begin, find out what is central to you as a person. Use a metaphor
  that reflects your identity to guide your practice. A colleague in a
  seminar described her teacher self as, 'A tree, firmly rooted in the
  ground. A tree that sparkles and makes others enthusiastic.'
- Instead of comparing yourself to others, celebrate what is unique
  and special about you. Remind yourself of the things you have
  already accomplished and appreciate your strengths.
- Get out of your comfort zone occasionally and try out new ideas so
  you can develop further as a person and teacher.
- Learn from others, but accept we are all different and you teach in
  ways that are authentic to you. For example, Sarah will never want
  to sing in class although she knows it works well for others!

Olsen, B. (2016). *Teaching for success: Developing your teacher identity in today's
classroom*. London: Routledge.

Plan your own professional development

> Engaging in self-directed professional development can boost self-efficacy, engagement and wellbeing.

One reason why many become educators is a love of learning. While classroom experiences offer learning opportunities, there are other explicit approaches to professional learning, too.

Continuous Professional Development (CPD) can be extremely motivating, boosting teacher engagement and self-efficacy; both of which are key contributors to professional wellbeing. However, it can also be frustrating and demotivating, especially when it is prescribed by others, perceived as irrelevant or of poor quality. In contrast, when teachers can choose their own pathways of CPD, searching out topics and learning formats which suit them and their context, then the experience is more likely to be positive. One additional caveat is that professional learning should never feel like another obligation and pressure. The key is to never lose sight of one's strengths and capabilities as an educator and to retain a sense of pleasure in exploring new topics and methods of interest and relevance.

You may find it useful to reflect on the following questions to plan opportunities for growth:

- What topics would I like to learn more about?
- What opportunities – alone or with others/online or in person – exist to explore this topic (e.g., online teacher groups, journals etc.)?
- When could I comfortably do this alongside my other commitments?
- What support could I get from my institution or colleagues?

Li, R., Liu, H., Chen, Y. & Yao, M. (2022). Teacher engagement and self-efficacy: The mediating role of continuing professional development and moderating role of teaching experience. *Current Psychology, 41*, 328–337.

Mercer, S., Farrell, C. & Freeman, D. (2022). *Self-directed Professional Development in ELT* [PDF]. Oxford University Press. www.oup.com/elt/expert

Richards, J. C. (2017). *Jack. C. Richards' 50 Tips for Teacher Development*. Cambridge: Cambridge University Press.

13 Plan time for hobbies and small treats

Plan in treats and savour them mindfully to boost your wellbeing and colour your week with positive experiences.

Individuals benefit from experiencing moments of pleasure and enjoyment on a regular basis. Research has shown that those who actively engage in hobbies as a form of self-care are less likely to experience burnout and more likely to be positively motivated in their professional lives (see 1). Being engaged in something other than work enables us to detach, and then to return to the classroom reenergised.

There are boundless possibilities of things you can take up as a hobby depending on your interests and what kind of stimulation you enjoy most, such as gardening, cooking, photography, arts and crafts, sports, knitting, dancing, chess, reading, music, collecting comic books, learning a language, etc. The main thing is that it allows you to escape mentally from work and become fully absorbed in something else. Fixing a date in your diary to dedicate time to your hobbies is key to ensuring that you disconnect and recharge your batteries regularly.

Another strategy is to plan small treats into your schedule. These are little moments of positivity and pleasure that are built into each day and week. Unfortunately, people often choose treats that are not actually good for them. These things may give a short-term boost, but they do not add positively to wellbeing in the long-term. Everyone enjoys different things so take time to really reflect on what would give you pleasure and maybe draw up a list to inspire you. Some examples could include having a short power nap, baking bread, going for a walk, finding flowers to brighten your desk, reading a book, listening mindfully to some music, doing a short yoga segment, etc.

Without it becoming an additional burden, try to make sure you set aside quality time to enjoy your chosen pleasurable distraction – big or small – both your wellbeing and ability to teach will benefit!

Sonnentag, S. (2001). Work, recovery activities, and individual well-being: A diary study. *Journal of Occupational Health Psychology, 6*(3), 196–210.

Using emotional self-regulation strategies can help us to manage our emotions effectively and stay calm.

Teaching can be challenging, and it is normal for negative emotions to pop up from time to time. However, letting off steam when we feel angry, frustrated or disappointed might mean we lose our students' respect, and we may be perceived as unprofessional. Yet, this does not mean we should repress our emotions; instead, we need to learn how to manage them rather than being overwhelmed by them.

Here are four self-regulation strategies:

1. Before a lesson, try to plan ahead, thinking what might happen and how you could respond. Use *if ... then* visualisations (see 87): decide what you want to do if certain situations arise, so when they do occur you will be better prepared to react appropriately.
2. On your way to school, listen to music or a podcast that inspires you, or read a good book. Before the lesson, try to build your positive emotions prior to class. That will make it easier for you to deal with less positive situations in class, if needed.
3. When negative emotions come up, think of times when you were happy, relaxed and balanced. Use positive emotion memories to counteract any negativity in the present.
4. In situations that trigger negative emotions, delay your response. Breathe deliberately slowly and count to ten – that might help you to see that more than one reaction is possible and choose a pathway that suits you better than your initial spontaneous response.

Mattern, J. & Bauer, J. (2014). Does teachers' cognitive self-regulation increase their occupational well-being? The structure and role of self-regulation in the teaching context. *Teaching and Teacher Education, 43*, 58–68.

Bracket, M. A., Palomera, R., Mojsa-Kaja, J., Reyes, M. R. & Salovey, P. (2010). Emotion-regulation, emotion-regulation ability, burnout, and job satisfaction among British secondary school teachers. *Psychology in the Schools, 47*(4), 406–417.

15 Use proactive strategies in the classroom

Learners and teachers benefit from proactive classroom management interventions.

Research has established that proactive strategies to manage classroom behaviour are more efficient than reactive ones. Teachers who use proactive strategies to establish clear class routines are more likely to pre-empt potential 'disruption, non-compliance and task avoidance by students' (Parsonson, 2012, p. 16). This helps students to stay engaged and on task longer. Pre-planned and intentional strategies can reduce behavioural issues and help everyone (including you) enjoy your lessons more. Proactive strategies prevent problems, are easy to establish, work quickly, and help make the learning environment more harmonious.

Proactive strategies work best when announced well in advance, so everyone is familiar with them. The routines need to be positively phrased and clear. They work particularly well when used in tandem with visual signals, as these help students remember them and this in turn enables the teacher to praise students for keeping to them.

Here are some strategies you could use:

- For activities, set out clear schedules with timings. Tell students beforehand how much time they have, and write up a countdown on the board, 'Time left: ... minutes', which you change as time goes by.
- In order for students to pay attention after pair or group work, tell them beforehand that you will raise your hand as an indication that the activity is over. When they see your hand up, they should stop talking and raise their hands too, ready for the next instruction.
- If mobile phones are banned in your class and a student is on their phone, you can ring a bell to indicate they should put it away.

Parsonson, B. S. (2012). Evidence-based classroom behaviour management strategies. *Kairaranga, 13*(1), 16–23.

> Perfectionism can contribute to teacher stress. It is important to know when your work is sufficient for purpose.

Satisfice is a portmanteau word that comes from the combination of 'satisfy' and 'suffice'. It literally means to do something in a way which is good enough. Rather than aiming for an ideal or perfect plan of action, it means selecting an approach which suffices for the purpose.

This notion is important for teachers who may tend to perfectionism and may set unrealistically high standards for all aspects of their work. Given the excessively high workloads that teachers typically face, it is important for teachers to set priorities and release the stranglehold of perfectionism. Satisficing is one way to do this.

In lesson planning, for example, there is a point at which any further tweaks to a lesson plan will make no meaningful difference to learning outcomes or to the quality of the lesson. While it can be motivating to strive for excellence, it can be crippling and anxiety-inducing to strive for perfection. Sometimes good enough will suffice. Additionally, overplanning can stifle a willingness to embrace spontaneous opportunities.

The following questions may help you to satisfice in your work:

1. What tasks need doing this week?
2. Which ones require excellence? (Certainly, not all – if that is your answer, you may need to look again with a critical friend!)
3. To what extent can you prioritise tasks according to importance and need for excellence?
4. What are the consequences if a task is not completed to the highest standards but is done in a way which is good enough?
5. For which tasks would it be enough to satisfice?

Philp, M., Egan, S. & Kane, R. (2012). Perfectionism, overcommitment to work, and burnout in employees seeking workplace counselling, *Australian Journal of Psychology*, 64(2), 68–74.

17 Tweak your job to make it more enjoyable

Job crafting refers to the small changes teachers can make to their job to maximise their enjoyment of their work.

Within the bounds of your job as a teacher, you will have a certain degree of autonomy which enables you to make tweaks to what you do. Customising your work in this way is called *job crafting* and can boost your wellbeing, job satisfaction, and work engagement. Although there are certain aspects of your job that cannot be changed, there are actions you can take to design your work so that it better suits your personal interests and preferences. There are three main areas where you can craft your job: tasks, relationships, and perceptions (Wrzesniewski & Dutton, 2001).

Tasks refer to the activities and responsibilities teachers have. Crafting could be limiting the scope of tasks you do not enjoy (e.g., set time limits on administration); doing more of the kinds of activities you like (e.g., bring in more drama activities); changing how you do a task (e.g., do marking together with a colleague accompanied by coffee and cake).

Relationships include social encounters with all the people in your job such as colleagues, learners, leadership, parents, administration staff, caretakers, etc. Crafting relationships means finding ways to have more positive, healthy social encounters and limiting the scope and number of negative interactions. For example, reduce contact with complainers; find ways to work with people who energise or inspire you; build in micro-moments of positive social exchange with everyone.

Perceptions are how we think about things, people, places and actions. Sometimes there is little you can change about an aspect of your work, but you can always alter the way you think about it. For example, see staff meetings as an opportunity to check in with colleagues or view tests as a chance for dialogue with your students about their learning.

Wrzesniewski, A. & Dutton, J. E. (2001). Crafting a job: Revisioning employees as active crafters of their work. *Academy of Management Review, 26*(2), 179–201.

Connect with nature regularly 18

> **Connecting with nature outdoors or bringing green life indoors can have positive effects on wellbeing.**

In the past, humans were closely connected to nature, green spaces, forests and animals. However, the move to urban living has severed that connection for many people. The *biophilia hypothesis* suggests that humans have an instinct and drive to connect with all living things in nature (Wilson, 1984). Fostering that inherent love of nature has been found to have numerous benefits for wellbeing and health (see **1**).

There are many ways to connect with nature.

- The simplest strategy is to bring the green indoors. Caring for a plant and seeing nature living on your desk or in your living room can have positive emotional benefits.
- For those fortunate enough to have a garden, gardening has been proven to have considerable benefits for mental and physical health, especially if the garden is biodiverse.
- Exercising in nature or just being outdoors can be beneficial such as going into the countryside for a walk, visiting a local park, or getting out on a river or lake on a boat.
- Even looking at pictures of nature or watching nature documentaries have been shown to support wellbeing.

In addition, if we can mindfully appreciate nature, we can amplify the benefits: smell the fresh air, notice the texture of leaves, admire the beauty of flowers, listen to the sounds of birdsong, and savour the taste of homegrown vegetables or fruits. A wonderful added benefit of fostering a connection with nature is that it is also likely to lead to a greater sensitivity to caring for the environment and the planet.

Capaldi, C. A., Passmore, H.-A., Nisbet, E. K., Zelenski, J. M. & Dopko, R. L. (2015). Flourishing in nature: A review of the benefits of connecting with nature and its application as a wellbeing intervention. *International Journal of Wellbeing*, 5(4), 1–16.

Wilson, E. O. (1986). *Biophilia*. Cambridge: Harvard University Press.

19 Take mindful minutes

Remaining calm helps us make better decisions.

Jennings (2015, p. 1) defines mindfulness as, 'a particular state of consciousness that involves awareness and acceptance of whatever is happening in the present moment'. This description evokes associations of the teacher being fully in the here-and-now of the classroom, remaining non-judgemental and observant of what is going on both around them and *inside* them. If you are not familiar with mindfulness practices, these strategies may help as an introduction.

- Take a deep and slow breath. Repeat this a few times and imagine that you're getting rid of negative energy as you breathe out, and taking up new and fresh energy as you breathe in.
- Before you enter the class, stop for a moment. Ask yourself, *What do I expect from this lesson?* If your expectations are negative, maybe picture some flower buds. Imagine giving them the warmth they need in order to start blooming. Let this metaphor guide you as you enter the classroom.
- In the staffroom, close your eyes for a moment – engage in some mental time-travelling that takes you to a place you like, that gives you energy, or calms you down.
- Do short mental imagery activities with your students. For example, ask your students to imagine – with their eyes open or closed – that they are somewhere else now, for example, on a beautiful beach. Ask them to imagine that they can feel the warm sun on their skin and hear the waves of the sea breaking, etc. This will help your students relax, provide some good listening practice, and can be used to develop speaking and writing. You will notice that such activities can have a calming effect not just on your learners, but on you, too.

Jennings, P. A. (2015). *Mindfulness for Teachers: Simple skills for peace and productivity in the classroom.* London: W. W. Norton & Company.

Arnold, J., Puchta, H. & Rinvolucri, M. (2007). *Imagine that! Mental imagery in the EFL classroom.* Innsbruck: Helbling Languages.

Prolonged exposure to stress in the workplace can lead to burnout. Prevention is better than cure.

Many professions, which are other-oriented such as education, are typically associated with a greater risk of burnout. Professionals need to understand how to prevent burnout occurring. However, if burnout does happen, teachers need to know how to recognise the symptoms and where to seek professional help and support.

Many of the tips in this section of the book are intended to strengthen wellbeing, buffer against stress, and thus reduce the risk of burnout. Identifying stressors, finding strategies to address causes of stress, being aware of one's own emotional temperature, and working with effective coping and self-care strategies can all help to prevent burnout. However, sometimes these approaches may not be enough. Over an extended period of time, a teacher can suffer from emotional exhaustion to such an extent that gradually they burn out.

Burnout is a psychological and physical condition that can occur as a result of prolonged exposure to excessive stress. There are three main characteristics of burnout: (1) extreme exhaustion, (2) depersonalization, distancing, or cynicism about one's job, and (3) a reduced sense of accomplishment or self-efficacy in one's professional life (Maslach et al., 2001). Those with burnout may feel emotionally drained, demotivated, frustrated, ineffective and lacking in enthusiasm. Physical symptoms can include digestive problems, difficulty concentrating, and disturbed sleep.

It may be difficult to distinguish burnout from other mental or physical health issues. As such, it is important to seek professional help to find ways to manage the situation and develop a pathway of recovery. If you recognise any of these symptoms in yourself, please seek out support.

Maslach, C., Schaufeli, W. B. & Leiter, M. P. (2001). Job burnout. *Annual Review of Psychology, 52*, 397–422.

Use a wellbeing checklist

> Try going through the tips on wellbeing to develop your own checklist which can ensure you employ important wellbeing strategies on a regular basis.

Some people know how to take care of their wellbeing. However, our experience with teachers is that most are so other-oriented in their attitudes and behaviour that they run the risk of not caring enough for themselves, while being dedicated to their students' wellbeing. After you have read the tips in this section, browse through them again or use the table of contents. Ask yourself, *Which are the tips that are most useful for me?* Go through the suggested strategies in those tips and draw up a checklist, adding your own ideas if you like. Referring to the list regularly as a prompt can help you to develop positive wellbeing habits, mindful of the fact that, ideally, self-care also needs to be accompanied by positive institutional support.

This is an example of how a checklist could look:

Develop my positivity:
- ☐ Add at least two artifacts to my positivity portfolio per week (see **7**).
- ☐ Check negative feelings before entering my classrooms (see **14**).
- ☐ Develop *if ... then* strategies (see **87**) as part of my lesson preparation.

Reduce my levels of stress:
- ☐ Engage in regular exercise – three times per week.
- ☐ Make sure I give myself three smart treats per week (see **1**).
- ☐ Spend at least three hours per week in nature (see **18**).

Build better social connections:
- ☐ At least once a day, have a chat with a colleague.
- ☐ Invite a colleague for coffee (see **10**).
- ☐ Do a random act of kindness at least once a week (see **5**).

Mercer, S. & Gregersen, T. (2020). *Teacher Wellbeing*. Oxford: Oxford University Press.

B: Psychological tips for leading with compassion, authority and skill

Teachers are typically the classroom leaders – they manage the relationships, group norms, discipline and routines, guiding everyone towards their learning goals. There are many ways teachers can lead a group, but the most effective approach is when they have strong classroom management skills combined with compassionate interpersonal skills to manage group relationships and work together with learners.

22 Start lessons quickly and firmly

> Get learners immediately engaged and thereby maximise learning time and reduce the risk of disruption.

The start of a lesson is a key transition in which teachers must gain learners' attention and get them engaged and on task. Research suggests that learners can spend up to six minutes in the initial time in class on non-learning activities, which can build up to five weeks of lost instructional time over the course of a year across all subjects (Saloviita, 2013). There is a clear link between engaged learning time and learning outcomes, so such a cumulative loss of effective learning time is important to address. The start of the lesson is also the time where learners are at greater risk of becoming distracted and engaging in disruptive behaviours.

Many teachers use the initial time to carry out tasks such as taking attendance or collecting homework. Here it can be helpful to set up routines so that these things happen quickly with minimal disruption. For example, teachers can place a tray on the corner of the desk so that students always place their work there as soon as they come in. Or everybody registers themselves present by offering a sentence revising a point from the last class, e.g., 'On Saturday, I played football with my sister.'

Ideally, starter tasks need to be linked to learning objectives and actively involve all learners. Some ideas include:

- Show learners images to tap into senses and awaken curiosity.
- Ask divergent questions or get them to generate questions.
- Write a series of words on the board and get them to think about what connects them.
- Use fast-paced activities: brainstorm 20 things associated with a topic within two minutes.
- Use movement (e.g., *true*/*false* questions – *true*: stand up; *false*: sit down).

Saloviita, T. (2013). Classroom management and loss of time at the lesson start: A preliminary study. *European Journal of Educational Research*, 2(4): 167–170.

A warm welcome can positively influence the classroom and provide information about the emotional state of an individual.

'Teachers who create a positive emotional climate for learning demonstrate that the classroom is a safe and valuable place to be and are enthusiastic about learning. As a result, students feel more connected and engaged in learning, and become more successful academically' (Reyes et al., 2012, p. 709).

The first few minutes of class are especially important as they can create a positive mood. Importantly, teachers can also learn how their students are feeling before the class begins and adapt their teaching accordingly.

Many teachers use some form of an emotional check-in system.

- Wait for your students in front of the class. Welcome them in a friendly way, greet them by name, and say something meaningful to each of them. (*Great to see you again, Leon. The story you told last lesson had me thinking for some time. / Hi Sal, I heard you scored a goal for the school team. Congrats!* etc.)
- Some teachers (not only of young learners) use a greeting ritual. They put up a poster on the wall outside the classroom, with icons or pictures showing a handshake, a high-five, a bow, a dance ritual, a hug, etc. – depending on what is culturally appropriate. When students arrive, they choose their personal welcome ritual by pointing at the picture, which is then carried out by the teacher and student.
- Older or shyer students can simply select a card from a pre-prepared pack of emoticons and leave it on their desk at the outset. They can be encouraged to change it during the lesson as their emotions change. This way the learners also develop more awareness of their own emotions.

Reyes, M. R., Brackett, M. A., Rivers, S. E., White, M. & Salovey, P. (2012). Classroom emotional climate, student engagement, and academic achievement. *Journal of Educational Psychology*, 12(39), 700–712.

Use language to facilitate learner cooperation

> We need learners to feel treated respectfully and we can contribute to this through the language we use.

Faber and Mazlish (1995) developed a model of constructive teacher interventions that can be used in stressful situations to show respect and invite learners to cooperate. Here are some adapted examples for ELT classrooms.

Problematic interventions	Interventions that engage students
Instead of using sarcasm:	**Describe the problem:**
Who's the smart one who forgot to add their name?	*Here's a text without a name on it.*
Instead of discouraging:	**Offer a choice:**
You still haven't handed in your opinion essay. I'll still be waiting for it a year from now.	*It's hard to start an opinion essay. Do you want to think some more, or do you want to talk it over?*
Instead of shaming:	**Talk about your feelings:**
I heard you misbehaved in Mr Brown's class. You should be ashamed.	*I was saddened to find out that MY class gave Mr Brown a hard time.*
Instead of criticising:	**Say it with a word and/or gesture:**
How many times have I told you to put your homework books on my desk before the lesson starts? Will you never learn?	*(Teacher pointing at desk, shrugging shoulders): Homework?*
Instead of giving orders:	**Give information:**
Stop talking to your partner. Be quiet! Now!	*After pair work, it's important to listen to me. Otherwise, you miss what to do next.*

Faber, A. & Mazlish, E. (1995). *How To Talk So Kids Can Learn – At Home and In School.* New York: Scribner.

Use positive micromessages with learners

> Often unconsciously, teachers communicate small but powerful messages which can be used deliberately to positive effect.

Micromessages are the verbal or nonverbal acts of communication that teachers send to their students alongside the teaching content. Often, such messages consist only of a single word, gesture or a facial expression. These messages affect the socio-emotional climate of the group as well as individual teacher-learner relationships. Studies have shown that, over time, negative micromessages can create 'micro-inequities' in a classroom, with students feeling excluded or under-appreciated. The impact can damage the student's self-esteem, self-efficacy and ability to make decisions in class.

The good news is that micromessages and micro-conversations can have a positive influence, too. Once teachers become aware of the subtle messages they send, they can work on using them consciously in order to engage all students and help them feel included and valued. Here are a few ideas you may want to work with:

- Be sure you know your learners' names and how to pronounce them correctly. Use them consciously and regularly when addressing them.
- Consider your facial expressions and eye contact, who you smile at and when, when you nod in agreement or encouragement and how you move around the room.
- Involve students in micro-conversations – these are quick short chats that can be about learning or their lives beyond the class. They help learners feel seen and valued.
- Take notes of things you have learnt about your students in those micro-conversations so you can refer back to them in future conversations. These bits of information are like social-emotional jewels – when learners notice you remember them, they will feel appreciated, included and will be more likely to engage positively.

Morell, C. & Parker, C. (2013). Adjusting micromessages to improve equity in STEM. *Association of American Colleges and Universities, 16*(2). From: http://www.aacu.org/publications-research/periodicals/adjusting-micromessages-improve-equity-stem

26 Task students with teaching their peers

> Preparing to teach others has positive effects on understanding and memory and can be used as a study strategy.

Research has established that one of the most efficient study strategies is preparing to teach. In an experiment, a group of students were asked to teach a text to other students, while a control group was asked to study the text in order to prepare for a test. Both groups were tested afterwards. The outcomes are surprising: the group of student 'teachers' showed significantly better results in what they remembered from the text, and in coherently understanding the text structure. The researchers concluded that when students prepare to teach, they use strategies that enable them to organize information more coherently. Although they are thus clearly aware of these useful strategies, they do not employ them in tests but do when they teach (Nestojko et al., 2014).

The findings can be considered in respect to language teaching. For example, tell your class that for homework they have to prepare to teach something to their peers in the next lesson. They can choose to address something from the present or upcoming unit – e.g., the content of a reading or listening text, a new grammar concept, an exam strategy (see **76**). They can first get used to teaching peers in small groups but as their confidence grows, they may feel ready to teach something prepared (and possibly tried out on a peer group) to the whole class. You can draw the name of a student or pair of students out of a box, or use a digital random name picker to select the 'teacher'.

Make sure that both the 'teacher' and other students get a chance to reflect on the experience. You may wish to explain explicitly the benefits of being the teacher. Repeat regularly so that everyone in class gets a chance to be the teacher.

Nestojko, J. F., Bui, D. C., Kornell, N. & Bjork, E. L. (2014). Expecting to teach enhances learning and organization of knowledge in free recall of text passages. *Memory & Cognition, 42*(7), 1038–1048.

> Experienced teachers use silence constructively and know how to deal with awkward phases of silence.

Bao (2020, p. 9) argues that the quality of classroom interaction should not just be evaluated by how much the students speak, but by 'the depth of learner engagement' including silent processing. He stresses learners should learn to appreciate the value of silence. He suggests consciously using observation and reflection tasks, which include moments of quiet.

- When asking an open question, it's often better to provide quiet thinking time. You can indicate that by putting your index finger on your closed lips, or by gently saying, *Let's do a bit of silent thinking before we discuss this!*
- At a convenient point, interrupt the lesson and ask students to stop, think for a minute and write down their feelings. At the end of class, students share their notes in pairs or with the whole class.
- Use memorization tasks, e.g., ask students to be silent and remember a text or a photo, remove it, and then compare what they remember.
- Use prediction tasks, e.g., show the beginning of a video. Ask students to silently think about it and then say how it ends.
- When students have an argument, it's often the more verbal students who have the upper hand in the subsequent power discourse, which can become emotionally heated with destructive outcomes. As an alternative, invite them to see how their perception of the problem changes after a few minutes of silence. In the meantime, ask them to write down their inner monologue and share that with their partner.
- If there is silence that is awkward or that you can't interpret, offer students a choice, e.g., *I notice your silence. Do you need a bit of time to think, or do you want me to explain to you the task again / give you an example, or do you not want to answer this particular question?*

Bao, D. (2020). Exploring how silence communicates. *English Language Teaching Educational Journal, 3*(1), 1–13.

28 Distribute your attention deliberately in class

> Ensuring learners feel seen and connected to the teacher is important for their learning.

Teacher immediacy refers to the nonverbal behaviours of a teacher which bring students and the teacher closer together physically or in psychological terms. These behaviours can include things such as smiling, eye contact, varied use of voice, gestures, relaxed body language and open posture. The underlying principle is that people are attracted to and engage with people they like and feel liked by, more than those where there is greater perceived distance. Research suggests that the learners of teachers with high immediacy have more positive attitudes to learning, better relationships with their teachers, higher engagement and, ultimately, tend to do better in learning overall.

There are two ways in which teachers can create immediacy, paying attention to all learners in class. Firstly, teachers can deliberately move round the classroom which reduces the physical space as teachers move closer to different learners in different parts of the classroom. Secondly, teachers can consciously ensure eye contact with all learners. This helps learners to feel they have a connection with the teacher and have been visibly acknowledged and brought into the group. If it is difficult in your context to note whom you have connected with visually or physically, then a broader plan can be used as a rough guide. For example, teachers can imagine the classroom as a five-point star and can even have such an image on their desk if it helps. They can then ensure they vary where they look during teaching, paying attention to each point of the star: left and right, up front, middle sides and back.

In online spaces, it is especially important to connect, such as by deliberately using student names and commenting on their responses in chat boxes or any visual cues (e.g., *Cora, I see your cat is helping you with English again!*).

Witt, P. L., Wheeless, L. R. & Allen, M. (2004). A meta-analytical review of the relationship between teacher immediacy and student learning. *Communication Monographs*, 71(2), 184–207.

Use measurable parameters in task instructions 29

> The more specific and focused task instructions are, the more motivating it is for learners to complete them.

The Zeigarnik effect is the phenomenon whereby people's attention remains on tasks that are interrupted. The implication is that we do not like to leave things incomplete. You will notice its use in productivity management and in online tools such as when you have a progress bar with a percentage to complete, a pie chart with segments to fill in, or a list to write with ten points. People are motivated to have all the parts completed or ticked off.

In teaching, this can be a useful strategy to get students on task and engaged. Firstly, it can be used to overcome procrastination and the initial hurdle of the blank page or a larger task. To do this, we can break down tasks into quantifiable chunks. Not all students will find this useful, but for those feeling overwhelmed, it can be a valuable starting point. If there is a text to read, start by getting learners to read just the first paragraph. Check comprehension, then move on to the second paragraph and so on till they feel ready to continue without the structuring. If they have a text to write, tell them to begin by writing the first five sentences. Once that is done, then they can move on to write the next eight sentences and so on.

When giving instructions, precise time and amount can also focus task engagement. For example, many teachers may simply ask learners to brainstorm ideas about a topic but changing the instruction to *Brainstorm at least five different ideas within the next three minutes*, will notably alter the focus, engagement and pace of the task. In task instructions, try using numbers that are distinct and tangible, e.g., *You have four minutes to write an email with six sentences to your friend about your plans for the weekend.* Using numbered lists and charts to complete also works to keep learners on task!

Reeve, J., Cole, S. G. & Olson, B. C. (1986). The Zeigarnik effect and intrinsic motivation: Are they the same? *Motivation and Emotion, 10*(3), 233–245.

30   Embrace the unexpected

> **Responding to learner needs and remaining flexible in teaching is a key skill for ensuring students stay engaged.**

Effective teachers are those who remain responsive to what is happening in class and willing to adapt their teaching plan to accommodate the unexpected. While good teaching involves teachers having a clear plan and learning objectives, classrooms are also unpredictable spaces. Sometimes teachers need to insist on their plan and rein in students who may be on a mission to distract everyone, including the teacher. However, there are also occasions where the best thing a teacher can do is embrace the unexpected and adapt their initial plans.

Adaptability is when teachers respond to learner needs, possibly by deviating from their original lesson plan. Learners may have different types of needs to respond to: emotional, cognitive and motivational. For example, learners may feel strongly about a topic in class, the school community or the news. Rather than trying to repress these emotions, teachers can encourage learners to use language to engage with and discuss the topic or issue. Some learners may be struggling to complete a task, so the teacher decides to add an extra step to scaffold it or asks learners to help each other. Finally, learners may be tired after a test in a previous class, so the teacher decides to begin with a high-energy task to get learners motivated and energised.

Here are questions to reflect on whether you wish to adapt your plan:

- Are learners especially curious or passionate about something that is worth exploring more (emotional needs)?
- Are there learners struggling with the task? Is there a need to add a stage, repeat a task, or provide additional support (cognitive needs)?
- Are learners motivated and ready to learn (motivational needs)?

Parsons, S., Williams, B., Burrowbridge, S. & Mauk, G. (2011). The case for adaptability as an aspect of reading teacher effectiveness. *Voices from the Middle*, 19(1): 19–23.

Negotiating learning contracts between learners and teacher can support positive group dynamics.

Learning contracts are a form of mutual agreement that can be negotiated and drawn up between teacher and learners.

They empower learners by giving them a voice about classroom life and involving them in democratic procedures. They help learners take responsibility for their learning behaviours and can boost their motivation. Additionally, they are beneficial for group dynamics and reduce the power differential between teachers and learners.

A learning contract can cover aspects such as:

- Defining behavioural expectations for classroom life and group work;
- Establishing routines for regular interactions such as registration or board cleaning;
- Forming rules about interactions such as listening to others;
- Organising norms for setting up tasks or group work;
- Determining timeframes such as due dates for homework and response time for feedback.

In the case of any disagreements or infringements, learners or the teacher are usually directed towards the contract by the others in class! A learning contract is intended to be supportive, rather than a restrictive corset of rules. It refers to both learner and teacher behaviours. The joint discussion about what to include and why is key to its success. Often learning contracts are displayed on classroom walls or in shared digital spaces. It is a living document to be revised and amended as required.

Lemieux, C. M. (2001). Learning contracts in the classroom: Tools for empowerment and accountability. *Social Work Education, 20*(2), 263–276.

**Provide strategies to deal
with exam stress**

> The more students know about stress and its causes, the
> better they can deal with it.

A little stress can sometimes help students prepare for exams. Too
much however, can cause anxiety, depression and even health problems.
Teachers can suggest strategies to reduce exam-related stress.

When students divide their time and set deadlines by which they will
cover certain portions of their study, it is less effective than if the
teacher sets clear deadlines by which students have to demonstrate (e.g.,
through practice tests or quizzes) that they are preparing effectively for
their tests (Ariely et al., 2002).

Knowing that there are clear, spaced deadlines can reduce stress for
some learners. Practice tests are also helpful if they familiarise students
with the exam formats so there is less uncertainty about what to expect.
Uncertainty is a major stress factor; hence, students should also be given
ample opportunities to ask questions about upcoming exams. However,
care must be taken not to only teach-to-the-test as variation in task
types is motivating and encourages student flexibility.

Regular reminders about how much they have already covered and
how few study packages are left can significantly boost motivation
and increase students' focus, especially close to the exam date as they
become aware of their progress (Katzir et al., 2020). A preparation
checklist to tick off milestones can make this progress visible.

Finally, it's a good idea to engage students in discussions about stress as
an inevitable part of exam-taking. Students can be encouraged to share
ideas for managing stress and preparing for exams.

Ariely, D. & Wertenbroch, K. (2002). Procrastination, deadlines, and performance: Self-control by precommitment. *Psychological Science*, *13*(3), 219–224.

Katzir, M., Emanuel, A. & Liberman, N. (2020). Cognitive performance will enhance if one knows when the task will end. *Cognition*, *197*, 104189.

Develop an authoritative leadership style

> Your interactions with your students influence your relationship with them and communicate your expectations of them.

Educational leadership aims to develop a classroom culture which students want to be part of. Such a climate stems from mutual respect, clear goal orientations and guidance in reaching those goals.

A leadership style emerges from a mix of high or low levels of demandingness and responsiveness. *Demandingness* refers to the expectations the teacher has and how willing they are to insist on those. *Responsiveness* describes the degree of supportiveness to learners.

Authoritarian leaders show high demandingness and low responsiveness. In contrast, *authoritative* leaders show high demandingness AND high responsiveness. They are 'responsive, warm and supportive. They are sensitive to a diversity of individual and collective needs and are inclusive. Authoritative leaders are also demanding ... they communicate high standards and [...] are assertive without over-relying on the rules and sanctions of the authoritarian leader' (Dinham, 2007, p. 35).

Good teachers will regularly monitor their own performance and make adjustments when needed.

- Observe yourself in interaction with your students. Do you tend to keep a balance between high demandingness and high responsiveness? Do you engage more in influencing your students, or exercising control?
- Invite a colleague to observe your teaching. Ask them to take notes of examples of demandingness and responsiveness in your teaching.
- Depending on the level of your students, you may want to ask them to give you feedback on how demanding and responsive to their needs they perceive you to be, and how they feel about that.

Dinham, S. (2007). Authoritative leadership, action learning and student accomplishment. *Australian Council for Educational Research Conference Archive*. Retrieved from: https://research.acer.edu.au/cgi/viewcontent.cgi?article=1001&context=research_conference_2007

34 Be authentic in your communication

> Being genuine in how we communicate with our students has a positive influence on their learning outcomes.

Research has indicated that there is a difference between *teacher authenticity* – the teacher acting in line with their own sense of self – and *authentic teaching*. 'Authentic teaching is perceived when teachers are viewed as approachable, passionate, attentive, capable, and knowledgeable' (Johnson & LaBelle, 2017, p. 423).

Perceptions of authentic teaching manifest themselves in teaching behaviour.

- *Approachable*: Use the time before and after class to talk with your students. This helps them practise their English in a relaxed way, while you can show them that you are interested in them.
- *Passionate*: Have a resources file or a folder where both you and your students share anything students find useful for helping them to learn English. Elicit ideas from students to add them to the file or folder.
- *Attentive*: Show an interest in your students' lives and wellbeing. If you teach several classes and find it difficult to remember details of what they share with you, take notes as soon as you get back in the staff room, and check those before you teach the class again. You can ask about their passions or follow up on things they told you. They'll notice your interest in them.
- *Capable*: Occasionally, put yourself into your students' shoes. Is your communication clear enough? Do you need to check by asking questions? Move to the back of the room and check your board management from their perspective. Get students to give you feedback.
- *Knowledgeable*: Keep learning. If you keep finding out new things about the language, new resources and original teaching ideas, it will show in your practice. Students will recognise and appreciate your continued efforts to learn and try out new things with them.

Johnson, Z. D. & LaBelle, S. (2017). An examination of teacher authenticity in the college classroom. *Communication Education*, 66 (4), 423–439.

Communicating learning objectives to learners can provide them with direction, purpose and a sense of progress.

Goal theory explains the motivational value of having clear, transparent and achievable learning objectives (e.g., Locke et al., 1981). Learners can benefit from the teacher making learning objectives explicit. Knowing what is expected of them can (1) give learners a sense of goal orientation, (2) make clear the purpose and relevance of tasks as stepping stones to an end goal, and (3) make visible a sense of progress as objectives are achieved.

However, as every teacher knows, some lessons do not go to plan! Sometimes learning objectives may need to change and be renegotiated with learners in light of experiences in class (see 30). The priority is to be responsive to the learners and learning taking place in class.

Reed (2012) offers a useful three-stage plan to guide the use of learning objectives and how these are communicated in class:

1. State explicitly the learning objectives at the start of class in student-friendly language. Use behavioural verbs depending on the level of the class such as *argue, compare, define, describe, explain, predict, summarize*, etc. (e.g., *Our aim is to learn how to write a narrative describing places using past simple and past progressive forms*).
2. Explain the purpose of individual tasks and how they relate to the overall objectives. (*You will pick a photo and describe it to your partner who will try to draw it from your description ... This task helps you to practise the language for describing places.*)
3. Remind students of the learning objectives (e.g., *We read the story about Luisa. What language did we learn to describe landscapes?*).

Locke, E. A., Shaw, K. N., Saari, L. M. & Latham, G. P. (1981). Goal setting and task performance: 1969–1980. *Psychological Bulletin, 90*(1), 125–152.

Reed, D. K. (2012). Clearly communicating the learning objective matters! *Middle School Journal, 43*(5), 16–24.

> Inviting students to share their identities can be inspiring – but we need to make sure they are willing to do so.

Herbert remembers teaching English to a group of 13-year-olds quite a few years ago. Among the children was John, a native speaker of English. To Herbert's surprise, John's level of oral production seemed to be on the exact same level as the other learners', apart from his pronunciation. Herbert's attempts to get more out of him were not very successful for quite some time. When he took John aside to find out why, it turned out John wanted to blend in with the rest of the class. It took time before John was finally comfortable to share his language more readily – very much to the benefit of everyone in class.

In order to help multilingual and multicultural students feel accepted in their new environment, language teachers often invite them to share their identities with their new classmates. Indeed, studies show that embracing the cultural knowledge and diverse languages of students can make it more likely for them to 'invest their identities in learning' so they can be more successful academically (Cummins et al. 2005, p. 38).

However, as in the case of John, the sharing of identities should never be enforced but respectfully facilitated on learners' terms and timescales. There are various possible learning opportunities:

- Students that have joined recently and whose level of English is perhaps lower than the group's could write identity texts in their own languages. Those could be translated into English and become a rich source of interest to other students.
- All students could give show and tell presentations about favourite aspects of their languages and/or cultures if they are happy to do so, e.g., a typical meal, tradition, festival, sport, a song, a poem, etc.

Cummins, J. Bismilla, V., Chow, P., Cohen, S., Giampapa, F., Leoni, L., Perminder, S. & Sastri, P. (2005) Affirming identity in multilingual classrooms. *Educational Leadership*, 63(1), 38–43.

It can enhance learners' willingness to communicate when they work with people they do not know well.

Willingness to communicate (WTC) refers to the learners' readiness to use the language they are learning in a specific context. It is influenced by a blend of personality traits and contextual factors including self-confidence, task, topic, the social setting and perceptions of their interlocutor or work partner. Unsurprisingly, learners feel more comfortable with people they are familiar with. However, there are also advantages to sometimes mixing up who learners work with.

For example, when students are overly familiar with work partners, they may feel at ease, but they may also become complacent and feel little authentic need to engage in communicative tasks. Working with partners they do not know well may create a genuine need to learn about each other. It has also been shown that if both partners make efforts to interact, each partner's WTC is enhanced, even when they are strangers. Thus, it can be useful for teachers to discuss with learners how to evenly distribute talking time ahead of group or partner work.

Below are some questions to decide whether to mix up students in partner or group work.

- How long has the class been together? Do they still need the comfort of working with a friend?
- Is the topic so sensitive they would feel more at ease with a friend?
- Is the physical setting relaxing or stressful so they could try working with a new partner or not?
- If the teacher chooses partners, to what extent can they be expected to positively influence each other?
- In this context, what interactional norms need to be considered?

Cao, Y. & Philp, J. (2006). Interactional context and willingness to communicate: A comparison of behavior in whole class, group and dyadic interaction. *System, 34*(4), 480–493.

38 Introduce autonomous learning in small steps

> Helping learners to be more autonomous needs to be done gradually so it doesn't overwhelm them.

Little et al. (2017, p. 267) stress that, 'Giving learners choice and making them accountable for their choices is an essential first step towards shifting part of the responsibility for learning procedures and outcomes from teacher to learners.' For example, Mercer and Dörnyei (2020) suggest a *choices and voices* approach. This starts with giving students easy options concerning the *how* of their learning first, and the *what* later. Trying to change too much too fast may indeed lead to frustration. Instead, a small step approach seems the best solution to start with.

- Give learners small choices first: *Do you want to read the text again before you write the summary, or do you want to talk to a partner first?*
- Prepare a learning plan for one or several lessons. This could simply include activities from the coursebook you are using with your class. Make clear the expected outcome for each task. Tell students they can do the tasks in any order and it's their decision whether they want to work on their own, with a partner or in groups.
- Include tasks that give students an A or B option to choose. 'A' could be about students working in pairs, changing a dialogue from the coursebook and rehearsing it so they can act it out to the class. 'B' could be about writing up a version of the same dialogue as part of a film script. Students decide on the film genre (thriller, romance, etc.) and adapt the dialogue so it fits the genre they have chosen.
- Ask students regularly to observe their own learning strategies, discuss what worked well for them, what didn't and suggest changes.

Mercer, S. & Dörnyei, Z. (2020). *Engaging Language Learners in Contemporary Classrooms.* Cambridge: Cambridge University Press.

Little, D., Dam, L. & Legenhausen, L. (2017). *Language Learner Autonomy: Theory, practice and research.* Bristol: Channel View Publications.

> Focusing on problematic behaviour is empowering for younger learners as it is something they can change.

T: *Stop being such a nuisance!* – S: *Me? I haven't done anything!*

This interaction is typical of what sometimes happens in classrooms. A student's behaviour has annoyed the teacher whose criticism triggers a defensive response – after all, who wants to be called a nuisance? Focusing on the behaviour rather than the person is far more likely to lead to behavioural change as a concrete action is easier to change than something which feels like it refers to the whole sense of self and person (Zenger & Stinnett, 2010).

If done in a non-judgemental way, action steps and a time plan can be agreed on. Here is an illustrative dialogue taking place in private between teacher and student.

T: *When the teacher tells a story, everybody should pay attention, would you agree to that?*
S: *I know.* (nods his head) – T: *So what were you doing instead?*
S: *Erm … nothing … I flicked my pencil on Sandra's head.*
T: *That's right. Why was that?* – S: (shrugs his shoulders)
T: *OK. Any idea how Sandra felt about it?* – S: *She didn't like it.*
T: *Any idea why?* – S: *I think she wanted to listen to the story.*
T: *So, what could you do differently next time.* – S: *Pay attention?*
T: *How does one do that?*
S: (shrugs his shoulders)
T: *This is how one does it* (gesturing). *Eyes forward to the teacher, ears forward, and freeze your body.* (Both laugh.)

The student, Mario, agreed to apply the strategy in the next lesson, and on a signal from the teacher as feedback. Mario's initial behaviour may have been an attempt to get attention – finally, he got positive instead of negative attention.

Zenger, J. H. & Stinnett, K. (2010). *The Extraordinary Coach: How the best leaders help others grow.* New York: McGraw Hill LLC.

40 Use celebrations wisely

Celebrations are an important motivational strategy, so it's worth considering how to use them most effectively.

Dörnyei (2001, p. 126) argues that recognition of success is important for learners of all ages, and regrets that classrooms are places where we continuously 'under-celebrate', thereby under-utilising a significant motivational tool.

One way of celebrating achievements is to make them visual. Teachers of young learners know how popular stickers can be to recognise students' efforts. However, students might become so focused on those rewards that they might cheat to get them or work hard only for the reward. Varying the things we celebrate is one way to counter this. One day we may celebrate the most creative text or one day the most well-structured one or one day the learner who made the most progress. This way every student has the chance to have their successes recognised.

Some teachers celebrate their students' birthdays. It's important this is done on the students' terms. Make sure beforehand that whatever celebration rituals you plan to use, they are suitable for the student concerned. More introvert students may find a public celebration uncomfortable and might prefer just a friendly chat with you after class or a simple note from you acknowledging their special day. Maybe offer the students a selection of birthday celebration style choices and let them choose how they would like their day to be celebrated.

Spontaneous celebrations are effective, for example, if your class has done something really well. Offer to show students a film, tell them a story, have a sharing photo session, take them on an English-speaking walk outside talking and identifying things in English, etc.

Dörnyei, Z. (2001). *Motivational Strategies in the Language Classroom*. Cambridge: Cambridge University Press.

Teachers can show learners they care by investing time in planning interesting and meaningful homework tasks.

Wentzel (1997) introduced the notion of *pedagogical caring*. It centres around how teachers communicate and show that they care for learners' progress and learning.

Learners identify pedagogical caring through their teachers' attempts to diversify teaching methods, provide individualized feedback, prepare attractive worksheets, involve learners' personal interests, and create tasks that are engaging.

One opportunity for teachers to show that they pedagogically care is in respect to homework. Sometimes teachers may use homework to finish up tasks from class where time ran out or by selecting tasks from the coursebook to progress through units. While this is understandable, if learners feel that teachers are not invested in homework tasks, it is not surprising when they feel equally uninterested.

In preparing homework tasks, here are some ways to show that you pedagogically care:

- Ensure tasks are related to the current learning objectives.
- Be explicit about the purpose and value of a task.
- Share your enthusiasm about it.
- Utilise formats which exploit resources beyond the classroom (e.g., flipped classroom tasks or learner videos of things outside of school).
- Integrate students' own interests, hobbies and passions.
- Provide a degree of choice in tasks.
- Let students design their own homework tasks!

Wentzel, K. R. (1997). Student motivation in middle school: The role of perceived pedagogical caring. *Journal of Educational Psychology, 89*(3), 411–419.

End the lesson deliberately and positively

> Ending lessons clearly and positively can reaffirm teacher authority and set up positive expectations for future classes.

As any teacher knows, the minute the bell rings, learners' attention will break and they will be mentally out of the door. In terms of teacher authority, this is a critical point when it is important to have learner attention to ensure the lesson ends on the teacher's terms. Thus, planning and timing for deliberate endings can ensure you cover all the content you need and retain authority by closing with a clear ending.

However, there is another reason why it is important to consider how a lesson ends. The 'peak-end' rule suggests that our memories of experiences are typically based on peak moments (the most intense emotional moment) and endings (our last emotional experience). Our memories form around highlights like photographs rather than a comprehensive recording of events. One implication is that if we wish learners to have positive memories of our lessons as well as positive expectations for the next class, how we end our lessons in emotional terms matters. We should make time to leave a lasting impression!

Keeping this in mind, here are some positive ways to end a lesson:

- Ask learners to highlight three things they loved about class today.
- Get students to stand up and high five each other giving examples of five things they learned or practised today.
- Have learners write a sentence about what they are proud of or happy about from what they did in class today.
- Ask *true/false* summary questions – students stand for *true* or squat down for *false*.
- Blackboard bingo – students choose five words from the board and the teacher gives definitions to recycle words.

Fredrickson, B. L. (2000). Extracting meaning from past affective experiences: The importance of peaks, ends, and specific emotions. *Cognition & Emotion*, 14(4), 577–606.

C: Psychological tips for the socio-emotional climate of the group

The socio-emotional climate emerges from the quality of the social relationships in the class and the kinds of emotions typically experienced by the learners in the group. It is facilitative for learning when learners feel safe, welcome and accepted in their individuality within the class, not only in respect to their teachers but, most importantly, by their peers.

43 Use *us/we* instead of *me/you*
44 Use restorative practices
45 Insist on politeness
46 Share something personal about yourself
47 Regularly take the group temperature
48 Share your enthusiasm
49 Be thoughtful about eye contact
50 Include tasks that promote kindness
51 Be aware of your emotional expression
52 Integrate tasks which require learner interdependence
53 Help students make responsible decisions
54 Diversify representation in your materials
55 Integrate whole group rapport rituals
56 Use ice-breakers repeatedly
57 Engage students in taking and switching perspectives
58 Use grading scales to establish trust
59 Use selfie wallcharts

Use *us/we* instead of *me/you*

> The language teachers use can impact the sense of community and shared group identity.

Language 'creates realities and invites identities' (Johnston, 2004, p. 9). Teachers are often the key source of target language for learners serving as models of language use. However, teacher language also impacts on the positionings of learners and teachers in relation to one another in how they talk, the words used and patterns of interaction employed.

Compare the relationship and power dynamics implied by a teacher who says: *You have to work on this task now before you can go to a break* with: *Why don't we finish up this task now so we can relax and enjoy the break afterwards?*

Teacher language can create perceptions of work/fun, obligation/ choice and learning/knowing, among others. In this tip, we focus on the potential strengthening of group identity and sense of community when teachers use *us* and *we*, instead of *me* and *you*. Obviously, sometimes the distinction remains relevant and necessary – you may wish to stress something is *their* choice; however, there are many instances where teachers can express solidarity and implied shared investment in learning goals. Naturally, such language use should mirror teacher actions, and students need to feel its use is authentic and welcome such a connection with the teacher. Consider the following examples and reflect on when and why you might use these:

- *Today we are going to work together towards the following learning goal …*
- *Are we ready to move on to the next task?*
- *Do we want to take a brief break now?*
- *How are we doing for time?*

Johnston, P. H. (2004). *Choice Words: How our language affects children's learning*. Portland: Stenhouse publishers.

Restorative practices provide powerful ways to resolve conflict and develop emotional literacy.

Restorative practice is an innovative way of improving group dynamics and reducing the risk of problematic behaviours: 'Centered on relationship building, Restorative Practices (RP), ... address antisocial behaviour by shifting the emphasis from blame and punishment to one focused on responsibility, accountability, nurturance, and restoration' (Schumacher, 2014, p. 1). RP uses strategies that encourage supportive and respectful behaviour among learners.

Here is an example of an RP format you could use. The *Talking Circle* can be used on a regular basis to develop the emotional climate and respect within a group. Only the person currently holding the 'talking piece' (a soft ball, perhaps) may speak. Everyone follows three guidelines: *confidentiality, honesty,* and *listening without interruption.* Schumacher (2014) suggests four possible phases: *checking in* (student briefly shares how they're feeling), *burning issues* (problems or concerns students are having), *topic of the day* (students choose what they want to discuss), and *closing* (e.g., making a wish for the week).

A version of the *Talking Circle* used for conflict resolution is the *Peacemaking Circle.* If a student behaves badly towards another student, a response may be anger, blame and punishment. Instead, this approach seeks to understand the feelings and thoughts behind the behaviour and how it affected all participants. It also aims to restore the relationship damaged by the altercation. To prompt a restorative dialogue, we can ask reflective questions, e.g., *What happened? / What were you thinking/feeling at the time / now? / Who was affected by what happened, and how? / How could things be put right?*

Schumacher, A. (2014). Talking circles for adolescent girls in an urban high school: A restorative practices program for building friendships and developing emotional literacy skills. *Sage Open, 4*(4).

> Politeness contributes to positive group dynamics and
> helps learners to work together harmoniously.

Politeness is a key social skill that has been shown to help children (and adults) earn respect, gain self-confidence, find friends and build stronger social networks. In classrooms, teaching and insisting on politeness can support the group dynamics and contribute towards a building of trust and respect. How to be polite may be especially important to address in online spaces where it is often more difficult to read interpersonal cues and where people tend to be have lower social inhibitions.

Different cultures have different social rules and expectations and you will need to consider what is appropriate in your social setting. Most social contexts expect Ps and Qs (pleases and thank yous), apologies when a mistake was made, an ability to listen to others without interrupting and a willingness to share resources with each other. Being considerate of other people, such as holding doors open or asking if they need anything when going to the resource cupboard, is also fostered when empathy is promoted such as through role play.

Depending on the age of learners and social setting, politeness can be addressed explicitly, incorporated into learning contracts, or explored as a theme:

- Teachers and learners can discuss together what acts of politeness they would like to insist on in their group (online or in person). Their suggestions can be incorporated into group learning contracts or added to a poster.
- Learners can keep a good manners journal, noting down examples of good behaviour and politeness they witness and wish to emulate. This can be used as a prompt for further discussions.
- Advanced learners can explore the notion of politeness in language by comparing pragmatic politeness markers across languages.

Croom, L. & Davis, B. H. (2006). It's not polite to interrupt, and other rules of classroom etiquette. *Kappa Delta Pi Record, 42*(3), 109–113.

Share something personal about yourself

> **When we tell other people things about ourselves, we build trust and connection.**

Self-disclosure is when a teacher shares appropriate stories about themselves, their lives, their experiences and their interests. This allows learners to get to know you as a person, but it also conveys that you are confiding in them personal information. This is valuable in building trust and respect, which are key determinants of rapport.

Obviously, learners are not interested in your entire life history, and you will want to keep many parts of your life private. However, there are aspects you may feel comfortable sharing, as appropriate. There are three aspects of self-disclosure to consider: (1) the amount you share – do not dominate or impose your contribution; (2) the relevance of what you share – it must be appropriate for the content, topic, setting and learners; and (3) the positivity – negative sharing, complaining or moaning can damage the perception of the teacher and classroom atmosphere, so choose the positive aspects to share while remaining authentic.

- In the language classroom, it is typical to work on tasks which require learners to share their thoughts, feelings or experiences – if appropriate, share your experience, too. For example, a student tells you that they spent their holiday swimming in the local lake and you could share how much you love swimming, too and where you go.
- If you use a selfie wall chart (see **59**) with information about learners, take part in this as well with a space for you as the teacher.
- Be open to allowing students to ask you questions – why not use yourself as an interviewee on a specific topic?
- Also consider sharing any struggles in learning and how you overcame them. Allowing learners to see our efforts in learning demystifies processes of learning available to them too.

Cayanus, J. L. & Martin, M. M. (2008). Teacher self-disclosure: Amount, relevance, and negativity. *Communication Quarterly, 56*(3), 325–341.

> Teachers need to understand the emotional climate of their classroom as this determines the engagement and wellbeing of both teacher and learners.

An effective teacher recognises the emotions permeating their classroom climate and the mood of the group. This knowledge comes in part from experience and learning to read the room, but it can also be gained explicitly. With a greater understanding of how learners think and feel about life in the class, teachers are better positioned to take corrective action if need be or build further on existing successes.

The *group temperature* refers to the emotional climate of the group as a whole as well as the feeling of individuals within the group. There are a number of strategies teachers can use to elicit feedback on this. Not only does this provide valuable information, but it also sends an important signal to learners that you are listening to student voice.

- Use exit tickets to measure group temperature. Pose three questions that students can anonymously respond to on bits of paper (or in an online poll) at the end of the lesson and you can read after class, e.g., *How comfortable do you feel in the group? What is the best part of being a student in this class? What aspect of classroom life would you like to change?*
- These questions could also be asked in a Google Doc, where students share their thoughts and can respond to each other. They remain anonymous but can see and react to each other's responses.
- Learners can be asked to share their feelings in class using visuals they hold up or just leave on their desk such as an emoji, a picture of the weather (cloudy, sunny, thundery), or simply a number 1–10 (1 feeling low; 10 feeling high).

Reyes, M. R., Brackett, M. A., Rivers, S. E., White, M. & Salovey, P. (2012). Classroom emotional climate, student engagement, and academic achievement. *Journal of Educational Psychology, 104*(3), 700–712.

> **When teachers share their enthusiasm, it is more likely their learners will be enthusiastic and engaged.**

Teachers can be enthusiastic about (1) their roles as teachers and (2) the subject they teach. When students perceive teachers to be enthusiastic about teaching, they evaluate their teaching as higher quality and more creative.

Enthusiasm about teaching can motivate learners by helping them feel that their learning matters to the teacher. Naturally, maintaining enthusiasm is not always easy, but some strategies can include:

- Engaging in CPD of your choice;
- Embarking on new projects such as doing a cooperation project with another school or doing a small-scale action research project;
- Taking the opportunity to travel and use the language;
- Trying out a new set of materials;
- Keeping a log of positive teaching experiences.

Enthusiasm for the language is another way to share positive emotions in the classroom. If the teacher is enthusiastic, there is a greater likelihood the learner will be more enthusiastic and show more interest through processes of contagion – emotions are literally infectious! A key to contagion is that the teacher clearly expresses and displays their enthusiasm.

Being an enthusiastic teacher does not mean leaping around shouting how much fun something is. It is about sharing your passions about what you do and teach. Having to enact this when you do not feel this way can be exhausting, so it is important to take the time to genuinely nurture your own motivation so that the natural consequence will be authentic enthusiasm that you can deliberately share with learners.

Keller, M. M., Goetz, T., Becker, E. S., Morger, V. & Hensley, L. (2014). Feeling and showing: A new conceptualization of dispositional teacher enthusiasm and its relation to students' interest. *Learning and Instruction, 33*, 29–38.

49 Be thoughtful about eye contact

> **Expert teachers use eye contact deliberately to communicate and to include all students.**

One way of building rapport with others is through nonverbal communication including eye contact (see **25**). Research has shown that when teachers use their eyes to communicate encouragement and show that they are listening, it can boost student engagement.

A particular aspect of eye contact and teacher gaze is how teachers and students can meet on a level with one another. For example, in a classroom where the teacher is walking around and the students are sitting down, a conversation held across such a difference in height can affect the quality of interaction.

Mindful of the need to consider cultural and contextual norms and expectations in your setting, here are some strategies to think about:

- When your students work in groups and you want to listen to their interaction without interrupting, make sure you approach them on their eye level. This might require you to crouch down, or simply get a low chair to sit on. Make sure you don't interrupt their interaction. Instead, use head nods, eye contact and maybe a smile to encourage them to continue with their conversation.
- If you want to talk to a student and there is a height difference, say, e.g., *Do you mind if we sit down over there so we can talk properly?* That will show them that you are taking them seriously.
- When you talk to the whole class, remember to move your gaze around and include all learners, while focusing eye contact to show your interest when listening to them when they talk.

McIntyre, N. A., Mainhard, M. T. & Klassen, R. M. (2017). Are you looking to teach? Cultural, temporal and dynamic insights into expert teacher gaze. *Learning and Instruction, 49*, 41–53.

Include tasks that promote kindness　50

Promoting kindness enhances group dynamics and equips students with a valuable skill for life.

The climate of the group depends largely on the quality of relationships between learners. In a positive group atmosphere, both teachers and learners flourish, and learners are more likely to be engaged and actively use language (see **45**). One way to boost relational quality is to promote and teach kindness. This enhances not only the relationships within the group, but it can also build friendships, peer acceptance and learner wellbeing. Being kind appears to help learners to become happy and liked by others, as well as to boost group dynamics. Naturally, learning to be kind to others is a social skill relevant beyond the classroom.

The array of benefits for learners were noted in a study by Layous et al. (2012) who compared learners engaged in three acts of kindness to those who visited three new places. Kindness won on every measure. For language teachers, attending to kindness can make your classroom a happier, safer place for learners to use the language, and it is motivating for teachers and learners to make the world a better place, too.

In promoting kindness, there are many resources online (see Random Acts of Kindness website specifically). It can begin with a discussion of what kindness is, highlighting the role of empathy (see **80**), and stressing that also small actions can be kind. Kindness does not need to involve money. It is more a way of being towards others.

- Have students keep a journal observing acts of kindness in others.
- Ask them to carry out three acts of kindness a week and report back.
- Brainstorm a bingo card full of acts of kindness. See who completes theirs first.

Layous, K., Nelson, S. K., Oberle, E., Schonert-Reichl, K. A. & Lyubomirsky, S. (2012). Kindness counts: Prompting prosocial behavior in preadolescents boosts peer acceptance and well-being. *PLoS ONE, 7*(12), e51380.

https://www.randomactsofkindness.org/for-educators

51 Be aware of your emotional expression

> When teachers use more positive forms of nonverbal expression, learners are more likely to experience positive emotions which will enhance their learning.

Emotions are contagious. *Emotional contagion* refers to the processes of emotional transfer in both directions between teachers and learners. However, as teachers are in a position of power in classrooms, this means they are especially influential for learner emotions. If a teacher demonstrates positive emotions, it is much more likely the learner will also experience similar positive emotions. Learners' emotions are known to be key determinants of their attitudes, engagement, learning behaviours and achievement. Therefore, if teachers can communicate positive emotions or at least manage the expression of their negative emotions, this could enhance learners' approaches to learning and their own emotional states.

Emotional management is related to the complex area of *emotional labour*. This refers to conscious efforts a teacher may make to manage their emotions to fit in with expectations of the emotions they should feel and display. If there is considerable dissonance between what they really feel and what they feel compelled to demonstrate, this can be a source of stress and emotional exhaustion. Therefore, this tip needs to be considered in daily situations as opposed to situations of particularly intense emotions.

In simple terms, if a teacher can verbally and non-verbally communicate positive emotions, learners will benefit. When learners are positively engaged and happy, this has a positive washback effect on teachers so that they too experience positive emotions. It triggers an upward spiral of shared, contagious positivity.

Frisby, B. N. (2019). The influence of emotional contagion on student perceptions of instructor rapport, emotional support, emotion work, valence, and cognitive learning. *Communication Studies, 70*(4), 492–506.

> **Tasks which learners need each other to complete can strengthen social relationships.**

In the language classroom, students are often expected to work together in groups. Tasks which require learners to work interdependently are likely to lead to greater engagement, interaction, cognitive flexibility and also better social relationships among learners.

A distinction is usually made between cooperative and collaborative learning approaches. Both foster interdependence. *Cooperative learning* typically involves students working separately and then coming together to share what they know in completing a task that requires input from all members of the group. *Collaborative learning* involves joint activity and co-construction of knowledge with students working together to understand and complete a task.

A typical example of cooperative learning is jigsaw learning tasks in which the overall task is broken into chunks to be worked on individually by group members. They then come together to share and teach the others so the task can be completed.

Collaborative learning requires learners to work together towards a common goal. Teachers may wish to assign roles to avoid strong students dominating. A typical example is a problem-solving activity. Common examples involve having to come to some consensus about what to do in a certain situation, e.g., *You are stranded on a desert island. What would you want to have with you?* Or, *You want to clean up your local park. What changes do you make or rules do you introduce?*

Tolmie, A., Topping, K., Christie, D., Donaldson, C., Howe, C., Jessiman, E., Livingston, K. & Thurston, A. (2010). Social effects of collaborative learning in primary schools. *Learning and Instruction, 20*(3), 177–191.

Help students make responsible decisions

Showing students how they can make healthy decisions teaches them important life skills.

Research shows that, when it comes to making decisions, teenagers tend to be more impulsive than adults; they frequently decide on something that offers the promise of a reward without thinking of possible consequences. 'This combination of reward sensitivity and impulsivity makes middle adolescence – from about fourteen to eighteen – a very vulnerable and dangerous time' (Steinberg, 2014, p. 83). Thinking about decision-making can also help foster empathy (see 80) and perspective switching, which can benefit group dynamics in class.

One way of raising students' awareness of the patterns of good decision-making is to have them discuss dilemmas. You could give them an example: *Imagine Tracey asks her friend Lisa if she can use her tablet to check her email. Lisa agrees. When she gets her tablet back, she notices that Tracey's email is still open and it lists a message with her name in the subject line labelled 'strictly private'. What should she do?*

Tell your students that in order to make a responsible decision, one needs to look at the problem from a wider perspective. One way of doing that is by asking questions:

1. What's the problem?
2. Are other people concerned too? If so, how?
3. What possible solutions are there to the problem (generate as many as possible)?
4. For each solution, what could the outcome(s) be for different people?
5. What do you conclude is the best solution and why?
6. Who else might be affected by that solution and how?
7. After considering that, is the 'best solution' still your final choice?

Steinberg, L. (2014). *Age of Opportunity: Lessons from the new science of adolescence.* New York: Mariner Books.

> Who is visible in our materials, and in what ways, matters to learners, their sense of inclusion and their motivation.

Representation refers to who is portrayed and how in the materials we use. If people see themselves reflected in positive roles, it is easier for them to imagine themselves in such roles. Equally, if they do not see themselves represented at all, they may feel as if they are invisible or do not belong. As Michelle Obama (2022, p. 93) says, 'In life, it's hard to dream about what's not visible.' Students will be more motivated to learn when they feel seen, recognised, and where teaching materials connect to their lives and incorporate their identities.

Not only do we need to ensure all our current students are positively represented, but also that diverse identities in the broader society and world at large are made visible to ensure we promote a culture of inclusion, openness and respect. Social groups and identities to reflect on in terms of representation include gender, sexual orientation, age, ethnicity, race, religion, social class, culture and disability. Which identities are examined in materials and in what ways will need cultural sensitivity to local cultural norms and expectations.

Teachers can approach their own or existent materials critically by asking themselves the following questions or doing this as an activity with more advanced learners:

- Which identities and social groups are visible?
- What roles are different social groups being cast in?
- Who is being assigned status?
- What privileges or advantages are individuals or groups assigned?
- Are any stereotypes being reinforced?
- Who is missing from these materials?

Such a discussion can be expanded from the materials to broader society and issues of social justice.

Motschenbacher, H. (2016). Inclusion and foreign language education: What linguistics can contribute. *International Journal of Applied Linguistics, 176*(2), 159–189.

Obama, M. (2022). *The Light We Carry*. London: Penguin. (Kindle edition).

Group rituals foster mutual respect, a sense of belonging and have a positive influence on the classroom culture.

Rituals are actions that get repeated regularly. They have some kind of symbolic meaning and create an inclusive classroom culture and sense of community. Rituals are important and help establish goodwill among the people in the classroom, which leads to classroom interactions 'characterized by warmth and respect' with 'higher levels of on-task behaviour,' as well as 'greater intellectual risk taking' (Diehl & McFarland, 2012, p. 326).

- Introduce a **gratefulness ritual**. Anybody can ask for this ritual when they feel they would like to express their gratitude to someone. The ritual should follow the same sentence structure: *Today I'm grateful to ... because ...* Make sure the expression of gratitude gets followed by a big round of applause each time. When the student has finished, ask if anybody else would like to express their gratitude to someone too.
- Introduce a **breathing ritual** to help students relax or gain new energy at a particular time in class or before a test.
- Establish a language-related ritual such as a **similes ritual**. At the end of the week, ask students to complete the following sentence: *Today, my teacher (the lesson / my work) was like ... because ...*
- At the end of the lesson, ask students to engage in a **thinking ahead ritual**. Ask them, e.g., *What things from the lesson will be important for you in 5/10/50 years from now?*
- Start one lesson a week with a **good news ritual**. Ask students to share something positive they have come across or heard about. Once rapport has been established, you may want to widen the activity to a **personal highs and lows ritual**. Often sharing not-so-good personal stories can create a lot of empathy and mutual support in a class.

Diehl, D. & McFarland, D. A. (2012). Classroom ordering and the situational imperatives of routine and ritual. *Sociology of Education*, *85*(4), 326–349.

Ice-breaker activities are designed to create positive group dynamics and can be used throughout the year.

Ice-breakers are short activities often used at the start of courses when groups are new. They help people feel more socially at ease with one another and can lower social anxiety. There are many types of activities that can be used as ice-breakers. Those which involve movement and some form of social information exchange are especially effective. For example, 'find someone who' centres on a list of statements and people have to move around the room talking to everyone and finding a person for whom each statement applies. Ice-breakers can be particularly valuable in online classes to bridge the physical distance between participants.

As appropriate, various ice-breaker or energiser activities can be used repeatedly throughout the course to bond the group, strengthen social connections, enhance psychological safety, and boost group dynamics. The shift in format is from introducing people to each other to building teams and social cohesion.

There are many example activities available online (see also Ur & Wright, 1992). When selecting one for your group, consider the following:

- If people already know each other, is the content appropriate?
- Is everyone active and involved?
- Are individuals sharing appropriate personal information?
- Have students mingled with peers they may otherwise not talk to?
- Can learners get to know and develop respect for one another?
- If it should energise, does it involve movement?
- How long does it last? These are typically short activities.

Chlup, D. T. & Collins, T. E. (2010). Breaking the ice: Using icebreakers and re-energizers with adult learners. *Adult Learning, 21*(3–4), 34–39.

Ur, P. & Wright, A. (1992). *Five-Minute Activities: A resource book of short activities.* Cambridge: Cambridge University Press.

57 Engage students in taking and switching perspectives

> Learning to see the world from different perspectives fosters empathy and helps students understand their own viewpoints and those of others.

Taking someone's perspective is about putting yourself into some else's shoes and seeing the world through their eyes. Switching perspectives is putting yourself into the roles of different people to see various perspectives on the same problem. These abilities help with relationship building because they create empathy with others (see 80).

In the classroom, you could get your students to think of a conflict scenario and ask students to roleplay it from the perspective of one of the participants. Then ask them to switch to the perspective of the other person. If you have groups of three, this could include a third perspective with the person commenting on the situation as a neutral observer. Finally, students could reflect on switching perspectives and how the conflict might be resolved.

Changing perspectives can also be used in writing (Seih et al., 2011). First, present a problem or controversial topic, e.g., a teenager wants to drop out of school to become an online influencer. Give students five minutes to write about the problem from the teen's perspective, starting with: *My decision is clear. I've decided to quit school, and here's why* ... Then tell them to write from a second position of a relevant other (e.g., a teacher, parent or friend) by continuing this text starter: *So, I hear you want to drop out of school to become an influencer. Well, it's your decision, of course, but* ... Finally, ask them to write from the point of view of a neutral observer who can see multiple perspectives: *I can understand there are times when ..., but I think it would be good if ...*

Seih, Y. T., Chung, C. K. & Pennebaker, J. W. (2011). Experimental manipulations of perspective taking and perspective switching in expressive writing. *Cognition & Emotion*, 25(5), 926–938.

Transparent grading systems enable students to see that they are given fair treatment in tests and exams.

'Trust is a critical factor as we consider school improvement and effectiveness. At all levels of the organization, trust facilitates productivity, and its absence impedes progress. Without trust, a student's energy is diverted toward self-protection and away from learning' (Tschannen-Moran & Hoy, 2000, p. 585).

One way to build trust is to be transparent about how we grade our students' work. Grading scales and explicit grading criteria can help learners see where their grade has come from and also break down student performance into comprehensible components. In the context of inclusive teaching, it is important to consider that, 'What is fair isn't always equal, and our goal as teachers is to be fair and developmentally appropriate, not one-size-fits-all equal. If we give a graphic organizer to four students who are struggling with text but not to their classmates who do not need it, we are still being fair' (Wormeli, 2018, p. 6).

Consider the following:

- Grading scales should show which areas of performance a student is awarded points for and how many points within that area.
- Students should ideally know before a test what they will be given points for, how many points they can get in total, and what the margins are for different grades.
- Students need to know they can ask you questions about your grading and correction system.
- If you use a differentiated assessment system or teaching approach, explain how it works and your reasons for using it.

Tschannen-Moran, M. & Hoy, W. K. (2000). A multidisciplinary analysis of the nature, meaning, and measurement of trust. *Review of Educational Research*, 70(4), 547–593.

Wormeli, R. (2018). *Fair Isn't Always Equal: Assessing and grading in the differentiated classroom*. Portsmouth: Stenhouse Publishers.

59 Use selfie wallcharts

> Selfie wallcharts can be an important mirror of the social-emotional development of a group's coherence.

Whether it's the cave paintings from prehistory or the self-portraits of the Renaissance, humans have always had a longing to create a picture of themselves and freeze it to help remember important events or times in their lives. However, it was the invention of the smartphone that has made it possible for anybody to see a reflection of their face and record it at the same time (a selfie!) (Walker Rettberg, 2014).

Using a selfie wallchart – a space on the classroom wall (or digital space) that students can use to stick selfies – has many advantages: it can foster interaction and sharing; can document the development of group coherence over a school year; can be used by students to make statements about themselves or communicate messages; can help students get to know each other personally; and can offer a myriad of stimuli for discussion and conversation.

- Ask students to create a short text containing two truths and one lie about themselves; the selfie should relate to one of them.
- Ask students to put up 'favourite selfies': in their favourite place, reading their favourite book, playing their favourite sport, etc.
- Tell students to prepare 'suggestion selfies'. They should reflect on a topic or an issue they feel passionate about and make a suggestion related to it. They can try to promote their idea.
- Present a quote to the class, e.g., *Winners are not those who never fail, but those who never quit* (Banksy). Ask students to think about its meaning, and create a selfie related to the quote.
- Ask students to post 'partner selfies' where they share a selfie of them with a classmate showing something they share in common.

Walker Rettberg, J. (2014). *Seeing Ourselves Through Technology: How we use selfies, blogs, and wearable devices to see and shape ourselves.* New York: Palgrave Macmillan.

D: Psychological Tips for Learner Engagement

Learner engagement refers to the degree and quality of learners' active participation and use of language in class. It is not just about how much they actively do, but how much they do this with heart and mind – having interest in tasks, concentrating and investing effort. Without engagement, learning cannot happen.

60 Engage students through prediction tasks

Prediction tasks are fun, engaging, and trigger a lot of language use.

Research has established that one of the key competences of the human mind is the ability to make predictions. 'Minds exist to predict what will happen next. They mine the present for clues they refine with help from the past … to anticipate the immediate future' (Boyd, 2010, p. 134).

Involving learners regularly in making predictions has several advantages: it is engaging because it gets them to activate schema and think ahead and it awakens curiosity to know if their prediction was correct or not. It also offers multiple opportunities for language use. There is a wide range of ways we can involve students in making predictions:

- Ask them to read a story – but only up to a certain point. Then, working in pairs/groups, they predict what's going to happen next. Optionally, give them six to eight words from the remainder of the story and ask them to use these words in their prediction. Students can also be given the title or plot outlines to predict from. The same task can be done with videos.
- Project a dialogue, line by line. At each line, ask students to predict what the next one might be, then reveal it.
- Search online for famous film lines, e.g., 'My mama always said, life was like a box of chocolates. You never know what you're gonna get.' (Eric Roth, *Forrest Gump*, 1994). In class, show the first word, ask students for their prediction for the next one, then show the actual word.
- Use a freeze frame from a film. Ask learners to speculate about what happened before and predict what will happen afterwards.
- Occasionally, in any lesson, stop and ask, *What do you think I was about to say now?* That can trigger a lot of laughter.

Boyd, B. (2010). *On the Origin of Stories: Evolution, cognition, and fiction.* Cambridge, MA: Harvard University Press.

Avoid overloading students with too much new information

> Managing the cognitive load learners encounter can help them to learn successfully and remain engaged.

Research has shown that most people cannot hold more than a maximum of seven chunks of information in their working memory, or use more than four chunks at any given time (Hawthorne et al., 2019). If the person concerned tries to handle too much information, the brain gets overloaded and blocked. Learning becomes impossible.

Cognitive load theory explains how learners will find it hard to concentrate and focus and are thus likely to disengage when they have too much to process and take on board. There are a number of strategies teachers can use to ensure learners do not feel overwhelmed by making the amount and form of new information manageable for them.

- Show students how to use lists, notes and mind-maps to distil key information, e.g., when planning a writing task or a presentation.
- Use uncluttered materials so students can focus on essential information.
- Make sure important aspects of language are revised frequently so they get stored in the long-term memory.
- Build cognitive load gradually by using scaffolding techniques. For example, before actively teaching a new structure, present it a few times in a context that lets students absorb its meaning. Then actively teach it by putting it into a meaningful context (e.g., a narrative) and writing some examples on the board, underlining the important part(s) of the structure. Make sure students understand the sentences. Give them receptive activities first. Then elicit the rule from them. Finally, engage them in productive activities.
- When giving explanations, use short, easy-to-understand sentences. If possible, use diagrams to support your explanations as visuals can be a highly effective way of reducing cognitive load.

Hawthorne, B. S., Vella-Brodrick, D. A. & Hattie, J. (2019). Well-being as a cognitive load reducing agent: A review of the literature. *Frontiers in Education*, *4*, 1–11.

Deliberately thinking about motivation during lesson planning can draw attention to opportunities to adapt or modify activities to enhance learner engagement.

As its most basic, motivational planning involves asking three questions about our planned tasks and activities: (1) Are learners actively involved? (2) Will learners find it interesting? (3) Will they feel able to do this?

A well-established planning model used throughout education is the ARCS model (Keller, 1987), which can be used when thinking about which activities and materials to use or adapt for teaching.

- *A = Attention*. Get learners' attention – use a question, a surprising fact, an ambiguous image – and make them curious.
- *R = Relevance*. Helping learners to see the relevance of tasks refers not only to life beyond the classroom, but it can be about its relevance for learning too. Sometimes learners understand why they are working on something, sometimes this needs to be made explicit.
- *C = Confidence*. Learners need to feel able to complete a task. Breaking down larger tasks into manageable parts can help.
- *S = Satisfaction*. Learners can derive this from a sense of achievement, teacher encouragement, interest in a topic as well as having some choice in respect to tasks.

Planning lessons with learner motivation in mind can help us reflect critically on how engaging our lesson plan is from the learner perspective. Naturally, in class we may have to deviate from our plan but considering the ARCS aspects as we select activities and plan our lesson can help lead to greater learner motivation.

Keller, J. M. (1987). Development and use of the ARCS model of instructional design. *Journal of Instructional Development*, 10(2), 2–10.

Use free-flow writing activities 63

> **Free-flow writing activities involve writing without stopping or worrying about accuracy.**

Students who get regular training in free-flow writing significantly increase their overall word-per-minute output. Interestingly, over time, free-flow writing can also have a very positive effect on the student's overall writing quality and engagement (Yasuda, 2022). It can reduce their inhibitions and students are often surprised about the quantity and quality they are able to write in a short period of time.

In order to inspire your students to engage in free-flow writing, tell them that some people find it difficult to enjoy writing because they worry too much about errors. Share the metaphor of the 'inner watchdog' that often blocks the writing flow because it would rather have them not write than write and make mistakes. Tell them to send it to sleep for five minutes, then write as fast as they can without stopping – not even to read what they've written so far. Tell them to forget about grammar and spelling, too. Tell them that only they will see the text they have written.

As most students find it very hard to write about absolutely anything they choose, you might want to suggest a topic or give them the beginning of a story.

When the five minutes are up, tell your students to write their name on their paper, and put all the papers into an envelope that you seal in front of them, ready for the next lesson, when you hand the texts back to their owners and ask them to read them. Then tell them to send their watchdog away again and start another five-minute writing flow to write a second draft.

Yasuda, R. (2022). Fluency development through freewriting and transfer to other more structured tasks. *Language Teaching Research*. Advanced Access. https://doi.org/10.1177/136216882210848

64 Make space for creativity

Incorporating creativity in all its forms can provide valuable opportunities for self-expression.

There are three approaches to creativity. In the first, creativity is defined as being able to think about an issue from different perspectives and generate original, innovative solutions to problems or dilemmas. Typically, it is fostered through problem-solving activities, research on personal passion projects, or the chance to suggest innovative approaches to familiar topics or tools.

The second perspective on creativity revolves around the use of the arts in education such as literature, poetry, drama, art, sculpture and music. The arts can be a rich source of materials to inspire discussion, critical thinking, prediction, perspective taking and interpretation. They can also enable learners to express their identities and feelings about the language they are learning in diverse formats. For example, students can be asked to draw how they feel about their languages and explain the image to a partner. They can be asked to look at a painting and describe what happened before or after. They can be asked to write a song about their favourite foods from across the globe.

Finally, there is linguistic creativity which involves the chance to play with language. Tasks can include creating poetry, making word games, exploring jokes and doing word games involving acrostics, anagrams or homophones, etc. It can also involve using multiple languages together such as getting learners to write a song or film script using all the languages they know.

Using creativity in teaching represents an invaluable opportunity to boost learners' life skills and engagement.

Comerford Boyes, L. & Reid, I. (2005). What are the benefits for pupils participating in the arts? *Research in Education*, 73(1), 1–14.

Maley, A. (2018). *Alan Maley's 50 Creative Activities*. Cambridge: Cambridge University Press.

How we introduce a task can set the tone and expectations of learners. It is important to frame tasks positively.

Imagine a teacher sighs and then says, *OK, I am sorry, but we have to do this. Let's just get on with it.* It is not especially motivating for learners and does not set up great expectations. Think also about the implied message if a teacher says: *If you do that again, I am going to give you extra homework.* Is this not framing homework as a punishment and something negative?

There are many ways in which teachers use language in class that send messages explicitly and implicitly about learning and our underlying feelings and thoughts about it. It is worth reflecting on how we speak in class and finding ways to remain authentic but be motivating for learners (see **24**). If teachers become conscious of the language they use, especially when setting up tasks, then they may be able to influence learners' willingness to engage.

Compare the following ways of introducing tasks and consider the effects on motivation, willingness to engage and persistence.

You now need to work hard on task 4. v *Let's explore the challenge in task 4.*

You must find captions to the following cartoon. You have ten minutes. v *Here's a cartoon. Let's have some fun coming up with funny captions. Do you think ten minutes is enough time?*

To become aware of your own teacher language, you can record yourself or get a trusted colleague to come in and note down the language you use. If you have an expression you would like to avoid using, brainstorm some alternatives before class and keep them visible on notecards on your desk to remind you.

Denton, P. (2007). *The Power of Our Words.* Turners Falls: Northeast Foundation for Children.

66 Use stories regularly

Engaging your students in stories is an enjoyable way of creating memorable language learning.

Egan (2005, p. 11) argues that, 'We use stories constantly in our daily lives to give emotional meaning to what would otherwise remain, as it has been eloquently put, "just one damn thing after another." Stories shape events into emotionally meaningful patterns.' From a psychological point of view, stories are more than just entertainment. They help us make meaning of the world.

'It seems that "learning without being asked to learn" – that is, when students are engaged because they intuitively feel that what is going on is important and relevant to them – neatly sums up what can happen when story meets mind, and comes close to the powerful effect that stories can have on your students' (Harmer & Puchta, 2018, p. 10). There are many ways to use stories to the advantage of your students.

Tell anecdotes regularly. They can be about almost anything: an incident you observed on your way to school, something that happened in your family or with a pet, a memory you have of the days when you were your students' age, and so on (see **46**). Then, when your students have listened to one of your anecdotes, ask them what anecdotes of their own come to mind. Students will notice that you are keen on sharing anecdotes and may share stories of their own believing they are not learning but, in fact, what a great way to get them using the language!

For homework, ask them to think about a story they loved listening to when they were a young child. Tell them to prepare it well in English, so they can tell it to each other in groups. Tell them a story that you were frequently told in your family. Share with them why that story has stuck in your memory. Ask them to share one of the stories from their family or friends. Give them the chance to write a contemporary version of a classic fairy tale.

Egan, K. (2005). *An Imaginative Approach to Teaching*. San Francisco: Jossey-Bass.

Harmer, J. & Puchta, H. (2018). *Story-based Language Teaching*. Rum: Helbling.

> Studies show that if teachers extend their wait time it engenders more participation, greater learner engagement and richer language use.

Teachers notoriously wait around one second or even less after asking the class a question – this is called the *wait time*. During that time, students need to think and process ideas as well as build the confidence to express that idea in front of others. Naturally, learners vary in how much time they need. If a teacher jumps in too quickly, only highly proficient learners will have been able to process and prepare a response. In restricting wait time, teachers limit the potential for other learners to take part. The silence accompanying wait time is a necessary and valuable determinant of student learning and engagement.

In a fascinating study in the language learning context, increasing wait time by only two seconds was found to increase student-initiated responses and generate longer, more complex and creative language use (Smith & King, 2017). A number of studies have also shown that a greater number of students are able to take part in responding when allowed a little more time to think.

When reflecting on your wait time practices, bear in mind that different question types will suit different wait times. For example, all learners will need more time to think and formulate responses to personal opinion questions compared to simple *true/false* answers to comprehension questions. In addition, waiting too long may feel unnatural to teachers and learners in the context of fluent discourse. You need to strike a balance that feels comfortable to you and your questioning context. In your next class, depending on the task, try to consciously increase your wait time to perhaps three or even five seconds and see if you notice any difference in participation and the quality of responses from your learners.

Smith, L. & King, J. (2017). A dynamic systems approach to wait time in the second language classroom. *System, 68*, 1–14.

Explain your rationale for certain tasks

> Learners are more motivated when they can see the purpose, meaning and relevance behind a task.

A key body of work on motivation has looked at it through the lens of *expectancy-value theory*. This proposes that two factors affect motivation: (1) whether a student thinks they can successfully complete the task (expectancy), and (2) the importance or relevance of a task for a learner (value). Essentially, there is a trade-off between perceived value of a learning task against an estimate of its likely success (e.g., *I think I can succeed in doing this grammar exercise but I'm not sure that it's very important or I will benefit much from it*). The perceived value of a task can stem from multiple sources: gaining enjoyment from the task; the importance of it; the usefulness of it; or the relevance of it.

Essentially, school-aged learners know why they are in class and that they are there to learn a language and/or pass an exam. As such, some tasks may not need further explanation as both teacher and learner know what is behind the task. However, strengthening the perceived value of a task can boost learners' motivation and willingness to engage with the task. For example, learners can discuss explicitly how a task will help them to communicate in the real world or how a task will help them achieve a larger learning goal.

An additional dimension is that learners often like to understand the *why* of an activity, especially if it takes an unusual format or asks them to do something they would not normally do. For example, learners may resist being made to work with unfamiliar partners; however, if teachers can explain why this is a good idea – its utility for learning, such as promoting greater discussion and helping learners become comfortable using the language with diverse partners – then the learners may recognise its value and be more motivated to take part.

Wigfield, A. & Eccles, J. S. (2000). Expectancy-value theory of achievement motivation. *Contemporary Educational Psychology, 25*(1), 68–81.

> Questions, which are face-threatening or inauthentic, are likely to trigger reticent responses or even silence.

Questions with only a straightforward right or wrong response can generate more silence than action from learners as well as considerable anxiety. In contrast, more open questions seeking opinions or with multiple responses can be less threatening and more inviting (e.g., *What would you do in this story?*).

Other types of questions are problematic for a different reason. They are unnatural. In the real world, we usually ask someone a question if we truly don't know the answer ourselves. Someone asking, e.g., *Do you know what the time is?* perhaps does not have a watch or a mobile. Their question needs a real answer. So, the key to making your questions natural is to ask questions that relate to a genuine information gap or an opinion gap: 'The effective use of questioning is not about "testing" rote-memorised answers but about using questions to get learners to think for themselves, connecting to prior knowledge and personal experiences, and reaching their own understandings' (Mercer & Dörnyei, 2020, p. 125).

Once we learn to reflect on these criteria for the kinds of questions we ask learners, it will become easier for us to ask real questions that challenge students' thinking and inspire them to actively share their ideas. Here are some examples:

- How do you know that?
- Do you agree with what … says? Why (not)?
- What examples for that can you think of?
- What would (most adults / young people from …) say about this?

Finally, we then need to strive for – and express! – a genuine interest in our students' answers to create authentic and real conversations.

Mercer, S. & Dörnyei, Z. (2020). *Engaging Language Learners in Contemporary Classrooms*. Cambridge: Cambridge University Press.

Pair learners to maximize effort

Studies have shown that students tend to work harder if they partner with someone who is working hard.

Working hard is contagious, and in order for that contagion to take place in a classroom, students do not even need to see what their partner is working on. It is enough for them to be aware that the person next to them is working hard. Researchers have called this psychological phenomenon *the bandwagon effect*, and are not sure what causes it. Possible explanations include the notion of *contagion*. This refers to the human tendency to (often unconsciously) imitate the behaviour of people around us – for example, when we are with someone who beams with positive energy, their enthusiasm seems to rub off on us. The key point is that other people's emotions and mental states can quite literally be contagious (see **51**). So, sitting next to someone putting effort into their language learning can indirectly motivate a student who tends to work less hard to work harder too.

Think about instances when you may deliberately want to seat certain students together to foster such positive contagion. Naturally, there may be reasons why students sometimes should choose friends to sit with. However, with some tasks, it is worth making a conscious choice to seat students together based on their likelihood of positively influencing each other on a task.

It might be a good idea not to share explicitly with your class your reasons for such a change in their seating arrangement as that might influence them so that they try to disprove the theory behind your decision! However, you may want to share your observation afterwards about their increased effort in working and praise them for it.

Desender, K., Beurms, S. & Van den Bussche, E. (2016). Is mental effort exertion contagious? *Psychonomic Bulletin & Review*, 23(2), 624–631.

Cold calling students can keep them actively engaged, and can provide teachers with a diverse range of feedback. However, it must be used with caution.

Cold calling or *nominating* refers to the technique where teachers call on specific students to answer questions irrespective of whether they volunteered to do so. It is controversial as there is a sense that students should take part in whole class discussions voluntarily as they may be anxious, shy or socially uncomfortable. However, there are also good reasons why its careful use can boost student engagement and enhance their sense of responsibility for learning. An additional benefit for teachers is that it may provide feedback from a broader spectrum of students than happens when teachers form an impression of the whole class based on the responses of a select number of volunteers.

There are a number of caveats to consider.

1. Cold calling must never be used as a punishment or to catch a student out for inattention.
2. It is best used in circumstances where there are low-stakes responses. Its use must be consistent and associated with encouragement.
3. Teachers needs to keep track of who has responded to ensure no one feels unduly focused on or neglected.
4. A compromise can be to give students coloured cards to put on their desks which indicate degree of willingness to participate (red = not at all; yellow = for some things; green = anything).
5. A teacher can randomly select students such as by picking student names from a bag or turning over name cards on a desk chart.
6. In the nomination, put the student's name last to maintain whole class attention, e.g., *What is the past of buy, Elsa?*

O'Conner, K. J. (2013). Class participation: Promoting in-class student engagement. *Education, 133*(3), 340–344.

72 Pay attention to the attractiveness of materials

It can increase learners' positivity, as well as engagement, when they judge materials to be aesthetically pleasing.

For teachers, there are two reasons to pay attention to the attractiveness of any materials they may create themselves. Firstly, *pedagogical caring* (see **41**) refers to the impression learners have whether teachers care for their learning or not. They are motivated and have high self-esteem when they feel cared for. Learners can feel pedagogically cared for through the care and attention teachers put into their materials and feedback.

The second reason stems from research on design and emotions, which suggests that when teachers attend to the attractiveness of something such as instructional materials, learners are more likely to experience positive emotions and want to engage with them. Think of a learners' response if a teacher hands out a poorly copied, old-looking handout with text only – this is not especially motivating or inviting. Instead, changing fonts, breaking up text with relevant visuals and including colour where possible, is likely to be much more engaging. The content may not have changed but its presentation has. Appearances matter.

Concentrating on visual aesthetics, teachers can make decisions about what colours to use, fonts, sizes, images, shapes, textures, etc. It is worth reflecting on how visuals can be used to convey meaning and metaphor. Any visuals used should reinforce learning and not distract. Beware of over-cluttering handouts. Remember that clarity of presentation in materials and board work can aid learning. It is also important to consider whether the class contains learners with special needs such as dyslexic students where extra visuals and unnecessary detail can make text comprehension more difficult.

Norman, D. A. (2005). *Emotional Design: Why we love (or hate) everyday things.* New York: Basic books.

> **Classroom decorations may have a negative effect on students' learning if there are too many.**

In principle, making use of the classroom walls is a good thing. For example, a textboard where the teacher displays the outcomes of their students' creative writing can boost students' self-esteem and motivation. The motivational and informational value of visual displays on classroom walls is one thing – cluttering the classroom is another. It has been shown that overly fussy classroom decorations can distract learners, especially young learners. In one study, the overall performance of learners at the end of the year in richly decorated classrooms was inferior compared to those in non-decorated ones. One explanation might be that cluttered classrooms cause cognitive overload and result in the working memory being unable to process effectively.

This is not a plea for completely sterile classroom space, rather a suggestion to choose carefully what you put on your classroom walls.

- Consider how often you refresh your classroom displays throughout the year. Tired and worn posters may be more dispiriting than motivating, but constantly shifting displays may become distracting.
- If possible, use the back wall of the classroom for displaying visuals that are very colourful and might distract your students.
- Use the front of the classroom only for visuals that might scaffold students' participation in class, e.g., verb conjugation tables.
- Having plants in the classroom may offer better focus than decorations that are too noisy. Including greenery indoors is known to be calming and can create a sense of connection to nature (see **18**).

Fisher, A. V., Godwin, K. E. & Seltman, H. (2014). Visual environment, attention allocation, and learning in young children: When too much of a good thing may be bad. *Psychological Science, 25*(7), 1362–1370.

E: Psychological tips for learner self-esteem

Self-esteem is how learners see themselves and how they feel about themselves. Their self-image is affected not only by what happens in school but by their experiences in all aspects of their lives. However, if teachers can strengthen and enhance their learners' self-esteem in the language classroom, there is potential for that to have positive spillover into other areas of their lives too.

> Holding high, positive expectations of learners empowers them with potential.

Teacher expectancy effects refer to the kind of beliefs teachers have about learners and how they can be communicated consciously and unconsciously so that they ultimately impact on learner behaviour and achievement. This theory was made famous by the 'Pygmalion in the Classroom Study' (Rosenthal & Jacobson, 1968), which suggested that when teachers' expectations were manipulated to have either high or low expectations of learners, this affected how teachers interacted with learners, and thus how learners scored on IQ tests.

Research suggests that when we have high academic expectations of learners, we provide more opportunities to learn, more detailed, constructive feedback, more challenge to stretch, and we engage more with such learners (Weinstein, 2002).

It is important to communicate high expectations for all our learners. A first step can be to consciously reflect on each learner in your class and how you treat them, even keeping a journal to raise your awareness:

- Ensure all learners are given the chance to share their ideas and express their voice. Keep a checklist of who you have engaged with.
- All learners need constructive, detailed feedback and encouragement which conveys your belief in their potential to improve.
- Work with learners explicitly on growth mindsets. This helps them to see you believe in the ability of all learners to improve.
- Monitor whether all learners are praised and disciplined with the same high expectations.

Rosenthal, R. & Jacobson, L. (1968). Pygmalion in the classroom. *Urban Review, 3,* 16–20.

Weinstein, R. S. (2002). *Reaching Higher: The power of expectations in schooling.* Cambridge, MA: Harvard University Press.

75 Ensure learners can work with their strengths

Helping learners to recognise and utilise their strengths can boost their self-esteem and enhance their motivation.

There are many different conceptualisations of strengths. One used widely in positive psychology centres on *character strengths* which refer to positive personality traits. One commonly used self-assessment tool for character strengths is called the 'values-in-action' (VIA) survey. Research leading to the development of this tool suggests that there are 24 main character strengths which are universal, grouped under six main categories: wisdom, courage, humanity, justice, temperance and transcendence.

The survey is available free online in different languages and also has a youth version. Completing the survey can be a first step in helping students to become aware of their strengths or simply used as a trigger for discussions on strengths including a critical reflection on the tool itself. In class, working on students' strengths can build their confidence, while also developing their speaking skills by:

- Sharing stories about when they used their strengths in the past.
- Reflecting on situations where they could draw on their strengths to help them in the future.
- Discussing how their strengths could help them with learning.
- Exploring ways their strengths can complement each other.
- Comparing ideas for using strengths in daily life.

The key is to recognise learner diversity and help every learner to see they have strengths which others value and appreciate.

Proctor, C., Tsukayama, E., Wood, A. M., Maltby, J., Fox Eades, J. & Linley, P. A. (2011). Strengths Gym: The impact of a character strengths-based intervention on the life satisfaction and well-being of adolescents. *The Journal of Positive Psychology, 6*(5), 377–388.

https://www.viacharacter.org/character-strengths

> Letting learners become the teachers can boost their
> motivation, confidence and sense of agency.

Hattie (2012, p. 88) states, 'When students become teachers of others,
they learn as much as those they are teaching.' To teach others requires
learners to understand concepts and display critical thinking skills.

There are numerous ways in which learners can be given more authority
in the teaching process.

1. Democratic leadership styles are when teachers share decision-
   making with learners. Students can be invited to voice their
   perspectives and vote for preferred options. For example, students
   can be encouraged to debate the advantages and disadvantages of
   classroom layouts and decide which they collectively prefer.
2. Students can form expert groups. For example, at the start of the
   unit, the teacher can identify five core learning objectives and each
   group chooses one to prepare additional tasks and input on. They
   can then teach their area of expertise to their peers.
3. Students can also become mentors for less proficient or younger
   learners. Teachers can bring two different year groups together and
   create a buddy system.
4. Sarah has utilised expert consultants in her language classes. She
   works with students to identify their strengths and areas they feel
   expert in. Everyone has strengths, whether it is locating useful
   resources, structuring texts, pronunciation, etc. When a student
   is having a problem in one area, they are referred for additional
   tutoring and support to one of their peers who is an expert in this
   area. Everyone learns from and supports each other.

Hattie, J. (2009). *Visible Learning*. London: Routledge.

Hattie, J. (2012). *Visible Learning for Teachers*. London: Routledge.

Stigmar, M. (2016). Peer-to-peer teaching in higher education: A critical literature review.
Mentoring & Tutoring: Partnership in Learning, 24(2), 124–136.

77 Use peer feedback for precise, constructive, positive feedback

Peer feedback can be utilised to strengthen relationships between learners, and it is also an excellent tool for learning.

By commenting on a fellow student's work, a learner can distance themselves from the text production or oral performance and develop a better understanding of assessment criteria. Once they appreciate these criteria in relation to a peer's work, they are in a better position to transfer those insights to their own performance. Peer assessment ultimately supports self-assessment and self-regulated learning. If structured appropriately, an additional benefit is that peer feedback can also build cooperation and positive relationships between learners.

1. Start with an initial class discussion of what makes good feedback – constructive, supportive, detailed, concrete and encouraging, which considers strengths and areas for improvement.
2. Present students with the task to be completed.
3. Have them discuss in small groups what the characteristics of a good final version of the text or oral performance would look like.
4. As a whole class, discuss and rank which criteria to include.
5. Have students discuss each of the characteristics and think of what that could look like in concrete terms (e.g., if 'structure of presentation' is one, they could reflect on aspects such as visual (opening slide outlining the structure) or oral markers of sequence (*firstly, next, finally*, etc.).
6. Draw up a table of these features including concrete examples.
7. Ask students to choose a partner to give feedback to.
8. Have each student complete the table for their partner identifying the strong features in concrete terms and areas that were missing or could be strengthened next time (see step 1).

Ngar-Fun, L. & Carless, D. (2006). Peer feedback: The learning element of peer assessment, *Teaching in Higher Education, 11*(3), 279–290.

Accepting that language learning necessitates making mistakes helps learners to be more willing to take risks in language use.

Fear of failure can hold learners back from success. Although some individuals may be motivated to make excessive efforts to avoid failure, many individuals disengage and withdraw.

If learners can embrace the notion that mistakes are a welcome aspect of language use, they will be more willing to experiment with language, and also gain confidence. Essentially, mistakes provide memorable and individualized learning opportunities.

Everything teachers and students do in the classroom creates a classroom culture in which mistakes are either welcome or they are not. For example, the sense of group support and acceptance is one key feature which makes it safe for learners to take risk in language use. The kind of feedback and responses from teachers and peers also determines how learners see mistakes. Everyone needs to offer support and encouragement so that mistakes become just a regular part of language use.

1. Discuss explicitly why learning and using a language requires us to experiment and try out new ways of saying things. Sometimes we might get this wrong. The key is simply to take note, learn from it and move on. Use the phrase 'useful mistakes' to trigger a discussion.
2. Get students to deliberately take risks in language use. For example, when writing a text, they can write any new words or expressions in a different colour – you can even ask for a minimum of five new attempts per text. These will not be classed as mistakes if used incorrectly but are a chance to experiment with new language.

Taylor, S., Eklund, R. & Arthur, S. (2021). Fear of failure in sport, exercise, and physical activity: A scoping review. *International Review of Sport and Exercise Psychology*, Advanced Access. https://doi.org/10.1080/1750984X.2021.1901299

Establish ways for students to feel useful in class

> Assigning roles to students can make them feel important and supports how well a class works together.

Studies have shown that, over time, certain specific roles tend to emerge in the interaction of groups. Many classrooms, for example, have a 'clown', while others develop as 'task specialists' (e.g., a student who is particularly quick at finding information on the web) or 'social emotional specialists' (students who go the extra mile to help others and make sure they feel included).

Dörnyei and Murphey (2003) suggest that rather than wait for such roles to develop, we could also proactively assign specific roles in order to help students understand that they have important things to contribute to positive classroom dynamics and are valued members of the group. Having a named position also helps learners develop a sense of responsibility and can create useful structure in class. Experience has shown that the assignment of roles can be particularly helpful for more introvert students who are often insecure about the roles they play in a class, and it can help develop otherwise hidden strengths in them. Of course, roles can be rotated regularly if students wish to try out different positions and responsibilities.

Depending on the students' ages, the roles they could take on might include *Time Takers* (who make sure that everyone keeps to the time limits you have set for tasks), *Task Reminders* (who remind everyone of, e.g., homework they need to hand in by a certain date), *Praise Givers* (who congratulate students who, e.g., work hard), *Group work facilitators* (students who encourage contributions from all members in a group), *Task Checkers* (who make sure everybody understands what they need to do), *Language Specialists* (a student whose job it is to ask tricky questions about language). Students may also have their own ideas of roles they wish to adopt!

Dörnyei, Z. & Murphey, T. (2003). *Group Dynamics in the Language Classroom.* Cambridge: Cambridge University Press.

> **Showing students that we like them and care about how they feel helps them develop a positive self-image.**

There are very few professions (if any) where empathy is more important than it is for teachers. However, although not everybody is equally skilful at sensing what is going on inside another person, it is a skill that can be developed.

'One useful way of developing empathy is to begin to practise listening to the feelings behind a person's words. Usually, we are so intent on understanding the verbal message that we can miss knowing just how the person is feeling' (Lawrence, 2006, p. 334).

As one way of practising our empathic skills, try delaying a reaction to what a student says, asking ourselves a double question, i.e., *What's the message I'm hearing? What's the message behind the message about how the student feels?* We often react to the verbal message and give advice to a student – while ignoring the emotional meta-message. It is the answer to the *second* question that can help us show empathy, by saying, for example, *You must be quite (annoyed) about what happened. / I can imagine that this makes you feel (excited).*

It may sound surprising, but one way of learning to show empathy is about trying not to immediately find a solution to a learner's problem. As teachers, we sometimes act upon what we *think* a student needs, rather than taking the time to understand from them what they really need. Once we know what the problem is, we can find out from the student what help (if any) we could give them. Sometimes being listened to and feeling understood may be all that is needed at that moment.

Lawrence, D. (2006). *Enhancing Self-esteem in the Classroom*. London: Paul Chapman Publishing.

> **Learners can be motivated by comparing themselves to and learning from role models.**

In language teaching, there are many instances in which L1 speakers of a language are held up as supposed role models of language use. However, in motivational terms, this can be a frustrating model to aspire to. Instead, seeking to emulate a near-peer is likely to be more motivating and represents a more attainable goal for many learners. Tim Murphey and colleagues have worked extensively on this in language learning and shown benefits in terms of self-esteem, motivation, enthusiasm, risk taking and amount of language used. Similarly, in social cognitive theory, witnessing the success of other people who are perceived as being similar to oneself can boost one's self-efficacy beliefs.

Teachers can work with learners to identify different types of near-peer-role models. These can be classroom peers but also people who share similar cultural backgrounds, people of similar ages/gender, etc.

- Generate a discussion on the characteristics of learners who would represent good role models within their class. Encourage learners to think beyond proficiency, e.g., looking at characteristics such as well-organised, creative, kind to others, witty, etc.
- Have learners identify role models of people who have acquired proficiency in the target language and who share a similar linguistic, cultural, or social background (e.g., actors, singers, politicians, etc.). They could bring in their biographies to discuss with peers.
- Consider having learners conduct interviews, podcasts, or videos with role models of people who use English in their daily lives from their local community or families to discuss their language learning histories and identities.

Muir, C. (2018). *Motivational aspects of using near peers as role models.* Part of the Cambridge Papers in ELT series. [pdf] Cambridge: Cambridge University Press.

Murphey, T. & Arao, H. (2001). Reported belief changes through near peer role modelling. *TESL-EJ* 5(3). Available at: http://tesl-ej.org/ej19/a1.html

> The relationship with parents is critically important in helping students feel connected to school.

In this tip, we are using the term *parent* to refer to whoever the primary caregiver is for a child outside of school. Although this tip is largely relevant for those working in schools, the ethos of sharing good news and praise with stakeholders is relevant for all levels of education.

When parents are involved in school life (e.g., attend parent-teacher conferences, respond to school communications, attend school events, etc.), children tend to be more engaged and feel a stronger sense of belonging to school. The relationship between teachers and parents is critical in constructing a positive space for parents to become involved in their child's schooling. Naturally, different parental commitments and prior experiences with schools can affect their willingness and ability to get involved. However, one thing teachers can do is make the school a welcoming space for parents by attending to when, how and why they communicate with parents. It is essential that both teachers and parents recognise that they share an interest in the child flourishing at school.

All too often, parents are either only consulted when there are problems or when they are put under pressure to support school activities. However, teachers can seek to keep open pathways of communication with parents and share positive updates of class progress as well as individual learner successes. All parents will be thrilled to hear if their child showed kindness to a peer, completed their unit of work on time, offered an original idea to a discussion in class, or volunteered for additional responsibilities. Teachers can enhance the teacher-parent relationship and boost learner self-esteem by taking the time to share the good news about their learners with their parents.

Miretzky, D. (2004). The communication requirements of democratic schools: Parent-teacher perspectives on their relationships. *Teachers College Record*, *106*(4), 814–851.

83 Encourage students to engage in gratitude practices

> When students consciously pay attention to things they are grateful for, it can positively impact learning.

Gratitude has been linked to a vast array of beneficial outcomes including enhanced self-esteem, higher wellbeing, lower anxiety, reduced risk of depression, strengthened relationships and better health. All of these in turn can impact learning behaviours. Getting learners to work on gratitude practices enables them to practise language and brings all these added benefits.

Gratitude practices refer to regular activities in which a person consciously notices and reflects on things about themselves, their lives, their environment, or their learning that they are grateful for and appreciate. It is most effective when gratitude becomes a regular habit and people have choice about their preferred style of practice. It is also important to note that young learners under the age of eight may not yet have the ability to engage fully in gratitude tasks.

- Learners can keep a daily or weekly gratitude journal or list about their learning or life more broadly – they can note down what they appreciate about themselves as learners, the tasks or topics worked on, their classmates or teachers, experiences, etc.
- A gratitude jar is typically made of glass. Every day for a year or semester, students write one thing on a coloured piece of paper that they are grateful for that day and add to the jar. When it is full or on last day of the semester, they can read all the things they were grateful for in the past semester.
- Students can be asked to write a letter of gratitude to someone who they are thankful for – this has a wonderful impact on both the writer and recipient. Indeed, teachers could model this by writing a letter of gratitude to the class using relevant phrases and expressions.

Layous, K. & Lyubomirsky, S. (2014). Benefits, mechanisms, and new directions for teaching gratitude to children, *School Psychology Review, 43*(2), 153–159.

Learn to read the signs of low self-esteem

A behavioural checklist can help us see which learners may need support in developing their self-esteem.

Mruk (2006, p. 104) states that self-esteem habits are often deeply ingrained and they 'shape our world in ways that are both subtle and complex, meaning that change requires considerable unlearning as well as new learning, both of which take time.' In respect to language teaching, Williams and Burden (1997, p. 101) suggest that, 'more successful outcomes are likely to result from teachers gearing their efforts to improving both academic performance and self-esteem at the same time'.

While we need to be realistic about what we as teachers may be able to achieve, learning to read the sometimes subtle signs of low self-esteem can be helpful in developing a nurturing and supportive classroom culture. Learners suffering from low self-esteem may use a range of defence strategies: extrovert learners can be boastful, even aggressive, while introverts may withdraw from any form of activity. Lawrence (2006, p. 1125) recommends using a checklist focusing on behavioural clues to sensitise teachers to learners who may need extra support.

- Does the student make self-disparaging remarks? If they do, you may want to tell them about famous failures – people who became successful in spite of experiencing failure at school.
- Is the student boastful? When a student boasts all the time, ignore their bragging. Try to change the subject – they will probably find it difficult to continue their bragging.
- Is the student hesitant and timid in new situations? If so, you might invite them to think what is the worst thing that might happen if they tried anyway.

Lawrence, D. (2006). *Enhancing Self-esteem in the Classroom*. London: Paul Chapman Publishing.

Mruk, C. J. (2006). *Self-esteem Research, Theory, and Practice*. New York: Springer.

Williams, M. & Burden, R. L. (1997). *Psychology for Language Teachers*. Cambridge: Cambridge University Press.

> Competition can be fun and motivating but if not used properly, it can create stress and disengagement.

Competition is a natural human tendency, and many students want to be top of the class or come first in something. The instinct is thus to assume that competition is a positive tool for motivation. Indeed, it can be. However, it needs using with some care and critical reflection.

In a competition, there is only one winner. Everyone else loses. For those who lose, competition may not be such a positive experience. Depending on the nature of the competition it can be motivating or utterly dispiriting. Some learners may feel left out from the start if they do not feel that they have a chance of winning, and there is a risk of mockery for those who lose. If students volunteer themselves for competitions out of class, this is a different issue and, indeed, competition in sports or public speaking can enhance confidence and help students cope with failure. However, in class, when teachers initiate competition, students have no choice whether to take part or not.

To ensure competition is used thoughtfully in class, it is worth considering the following points:

- Consider what the chances are for everyone to win. Vary the criteria of the competition so everyone has a chance of winning. For example, who has the most original idea to solve a problem or who has accompanied a text with the most powerful visual or who has used the most items of new vocabulary from the unit?
- Have the possibility for multiple winners or do team competitions so as not to isolate individuals.
- Try to focus also on the process of doing a task and not just on the product or outcome (e.g., *How did you do that so efficiently?*).
- Reflect on whether a cooperative approach to a task might be a better option than competition.

Shindler, J. (2010). *Transformative Classroom Management: Positive strategies to engage all students and promote a psychology of success.* San Francisco, CA: Jossey-Bass.

F: Psychological tips for empowering learners

Empowering learners means giving them voice, a sense of control, and a feeling that they can make a positive difference to their learning. When teachers empower learners, they enable them to take an active role in directing what and how they learn.

86 Help students break long-term goals into short-term ones

87 Show students how to use *if ... then* strategies to reach goals

88 Make learning progress visible

89 Give questioning over to students

90 Help learners understand their role in achievement

91 Inspire your students to engage in deliberate practice

92 Welcome desirable difficulty

93 Praise effort and process, not product and person

94 Prompt students to be proactive about their learning

95 Show students how drawing can enhance their learning

96 Build in brain breaks

97 View feedback as a dialogue

98 Encourage your students to keep a portfolio

99 Help students learn how to learn

100 Embrace all learners' languages

101 Integrate life skills

86 Help students break long-term goals into short-term ones

Students may feel overwhelmed by complex long-term goals. Help them set short-term goals in addition.

The behavioural science literature shows that goal setting significantly increases performance compared to an approach where students are simply told to do their best. However, if the goals are long-term and complex, such as, for example, *I would like to gain some work experience in an English-speaking country*, teachers need to give students additional support to help them reach such goals. This is because long-term and complex goals may feel unattainable and it is hard to feel a sense of progress, which can lead to loss of motivation. In contrast, short-term goals offer more opportunities to check progress and gain a sense of achievement, which in turn can boost students' work morale. They also enable students to try a different strategy more readily if they notice that they are not successful in achieving a short-term goal before it is too late.

- Talk to your students about their learning goals. Ask them to share their goals and discuss whether they are more short- or long-term goals, and reflect on how easy they are to achieve and why.
- Ask them to categorise the reasons.
- Working with their reasons, explain that long-term goals are best supported with additional short-term goals.
- Challenge them to break up their long-term goals into short term ones without losing sight of the long-term goal. Make sure the goals are concrete and have clear progression-markers to ensure a sense of progress. *I want to study harder*, for example, doesn't have clear progress markers in contrast to: *I'll set aside 20 minutes each day to test myself on at least 20 of the new words we are learning in the lessons so that I'm better prepared for the next vocabulary test.*

Latham, G. P. & Seijts, G. H. (1999). The effects of proximal and distal goals on performance on a moderately complex task. *Journal of Organizational Behavior, 20*(4), 421–429.

Thinking about concrete strategies in relation to goals can help students to have a clear pathway of action.

Studies have shown that a combination of two cognitive strategies – *mental contrasting* and *implementation intentions* – can bring about significant improvements for both adolescent and adult students in keeping long-term goals in sight while working towards achieving them (Duckworth et al., 2011).

To engage students in mental contrasting, invite them to envision what it would be like to achieve a certain long-term goal and compare it mentally with the present situation or the possibility that they do not achieve the goal. 'Mental contrasting energises individuals to take action and strengthens their goal' (Duckworth et al., 2011, p. 18). The mere formulation of goals is often insufficient to ensure successful action.

Along with having a clear mental vision, students can work on developing their implementation intentions. These are planned actions to overcome procrastination or obstacles which might hinder them achieving their goals. Ask your students to envisage what kind of problems might come up that could stop them from taking the actions needed to work towards their goals. Then have them formulate three concrete *if ... then* strategies to overcome those hurdles. For example: *If I keep postponing making a short video of myself talking English, then I'll set my alarm 15 minutes earlier tomorrow and record it first thing!*

Once students have become familiar with thinking through such scenarios and strategies, it's a good idea to ask them regularly to report in class on how they are progressing and reflect on how well the strategies work for them and whether any other ideas may be worth exploring.

Duckworth, A. L., Grant, H., Loew, B., Oettingen, G. & Gollwitzer, P. M. (2011). Self-regulation strategies improve self-discipline in adolescents: Benefits of mental contrasting and implementation intentions. *Educational Psychology*, *31*(1), 17–26.

88 Make learning progress visible

> Helping learners become aware of their progress is important for their sense of confidence and motivation.

'Language learning is a slow, incremental process, and gains can be hard to detect for both teachers and learners. In order to develop a sense of competence, learners need to be able to see that they are improving and that their efforts are worthwhile' (Mercer & Dörnyei, 2020, p. 42). When learners become aware of their progress, it can enhance their confidence and also boosts their motivation and willingness to keep investing in the language learning process.

There are a number of ways in which learners can be made aware of their progress. In classes where coursebooks are used, Sarah has had students turn to the last chapter at the start of the year and just spend five minutes exploring it. She then makes a promise that they will all be able to cope with that chapter by the end of the year, despite currently feeling perhaps a little overwhelmed by it – a promise that can be displayed in class if appropriate. At the end of the year, when the class starts work on that chapter, they all make note of how much they have learned and how much more they can do in that chapter compared to the start of the year.

On a smaller timescale, teachers can use exit tickets for learners to write down what they learned that lesson. A unit can be framed with can-do statements (such as those used in many coursebooks based on CEFR) which can be examined at the start and end of a unit. Students can also keep a portfolio of work to witness their own growth and development.

Learners can also be encouraged to set short-term goals expressed in explicit terms such as SMART goals (Specific; Measurable; Achievable; Relevant; Time-bound). These are goals which can easily be identified as completed and ticked off – again making their progress and growth visible. (For example, *By the end of this month, I will have completed four of the twelve additional tasks in the workbook.*)

Mercer, S. & Dörnyei, Z. (2020). *Engaging Language Learners in Contemporary Classrooms*. Cambridge: Cambridge University Press.

Empowering students to ask questions enhances their confidence, engagement and critical thinking.

Typically, in teaching, teachers are the ones who ask the questions and learners respond. One small change that teachers can make is to get learners to be the ones to ask questions. This stimulates their thinking skills, boosts their confidence, and puts them in control of the direction of learning in class (Rothstein & Santana, 2011). Below are four ideas:

1. In a group discussion, the teacher can trigger a first question about a pre-established topic and then pass the ball (literally or metaphorically!) to a learner in class who answers that question and then poses another to a peer who then takes up the ball. The challenge is to keep the question-and-answer chain going among the learners for as long as possible.

2. Learners generate as many questions as possible on a specific topic or theme. To begin, they brainstorm possible questions in small groups. There should be no restrictions or exclusion at this stage. The next step is for two groups to meet and share questions. Together, they make a shortlist, prioritising the most interesting and worthwhile questions for the whole class to explore.

3. Students form small groups. All groups are given the same reading text but with no questions. They are asked to prepare, e.g., five comprehension questions and two divergent (open-ended or opinion) questions for another group to answer. They swap questions, prepare their answers, and then meet up to exchange their answers and discuss their questions. Some students will need help with this format at the beginning, but it can soon become a habit and style they are familiar with.

4. Ask students – either individually or in small groups – to brainstorm questions about a forthcoming syllabus item, e.g., a grammar point, and use their questions to teach the point in question (see **26**).

Rothstein, D. & Santana, L. (2011). *Make Just One Change: Teach students to ask their own questions*. Cambridge: Harvard Education Press.

Help learners understand their role in achievement

> Learners taking ownership of their successes and failures empowers them with control for the future.

Attribution theory (Weiner, 1992) is concerned with how learners explain their successes and failures to themselves and others. In other words, what do they attribute their achievement to? What reasons do they give for their learning outcomes?

Attributions centre around three characteristics: locus of control, stability, and controllability. The *locus of control* refers to whether you feel the reason was something within you (internal) or external. *Stability* refers to whether you feel that the thing is stable or can change over time. *Controllability* is concerned with the degree to which you feel you can control the reason identified. For example, effort is internal, unstable and within your control. Such attributions are empowering in the long-term as it places your achievement within your sphere of influence. Luck, in contrast, is external, unstable and uncontrollable.

If students receive test scores, they can be asked to reflect explicitly on these questions with teacher guidance:

1. Did you expect this result? Why/why not?
2. Why do you think you got this result?
3. What could you do next time to improve on this test result?
4. What concrete steps will you take from now on to take control of your test score?
5. What support from me, your peers, or other resources can you draw on?

Sometimes students may attribute successes to luck, or failures to a perceived lack of ability (conceptualised as an unchangeable and uncontrollable factor). They may vary across cultural contexts and genders. In such cases, teachers may want to hold explicit group discussions. A sense of control, also needs to be accompanied by concrete suggestions of strategies and pathways of action.

Weiner, B. (1992). *Human Motivation: Metaphors, theories, and research*. Newbury Park: Sage.

To learn skills well, students need to practise with deliberate focus and concentration.

The term *practice* can lead to mindless repetition which, in spite of best intentions, may fail to notably improve performance. *Deliberate* or *purposeful practice* is a different form of practice. It is based on a series of intentional steps derived from study of how top performers in areas such as sports, music and science have developed their capabilities.

Ericsson and Pool (2016, pp. 152–153) describe how multiple Olympic gold medallist Natalie Coughlin realized that she needed to focus her mind as well as her body. Her performance improved dramatically. She described how she tried 'to make each stroke as close to perfect as possible [...] figuring out exactly how her body feels during a 'perfect stroke' [...] and then work on ways to keep her strokes as close to ideal as possible.'

There are five main stages of deliberate practice which can be employed in any skill development: (1) break down the skill you are learning into component parts; (2) identify the part you need to work more on; (3) set goals and find strategies for repeatedly practising this specific part paying attention to details of your performance; (4) seek feedback from others and use this to refine your practice; (5) try putting the component you have deliberately practised back into overall performance.

- Ask learners to **search for one area they want to improve**.
- Ask them to **engage in deliberate and focused practice**. They could, e.g., watch the same film again and again, first with subtitles, later covering them up, until their understanding becomes fluent.
- Make clear that **focused attention is crucial**, and it's better to work in a fully concentrated way for a **shorter period of time** than at 70 percent of more mindless effort for a longer time.

Ericsson, A. & Pool, R. (2016). *Peak: Secrets from the new science of expertise.* New York: Houghton Mifflin Harcourt.

92 Welcome desirable difficulty

> **Finding the right level of challenge and difficulty can support learner engagement and boost confidence.**

Leslie (2014) uses the term *desirable difficulty* to convey the notion that it is desirable for learners to experience some difficulty in learning. Feeling challenged and having to expend effort in learning is more engaging and learners are more likely to remember what they have made efforts to learn. A hard-earned success has more meaning than one that feels too easy.

Puchta and Williams (2011) also draw attention to the challenge of keeping language simple but without dumbing down the thinking required from learners. One way to enhance the difficulty of tasks is to add cognitively challenging elements such as creativity and critical thinking. For example, learners can compare similarities and differences between cats and dogs, thinking more deeply about the topic but using manageable language forms.

- Inductive approaches to learning grammar can also provide challenge. Students can investigate examples of language and try to deduce what the rule is.
- Problem-based learning enables learners to explore open-ended problems for which there are no clear, simple solutions. For example, learners could reflect on strategies to tackle an environmental issue such as how to locally enhance biodiversity.

The key is to actively design activities so that they comprise a desirable level of difficulty in terms of cognition for all learners while remaining manageable.

Leslie, I. (2014). *Curious: The desire to know and why your future depends on it.* London: Quercus.

Puchta, H. & Williams, M. (2011). *Teaching Young Learners to Think.* Innsbruck: Helbling Languages.

Praise effort and process, not product and person

> Praising learners' effort makes them more prepared to engage fully in their learning.

Most teachers would agree that praise is an important educational strategy. After all, everyone wants to hear positive messages about themselves, and you might well assume that in a book with psychological tips, praise would rank very highly – or would it?

Let's look at an experiment. Hundreds of students were given ten challenging cognitive tasks. Half of them were then praised for ability (e.g., *You have real talent – 9 out of 10. You're great!*), the other half for effort (e.g., *You got 9 of 10. You must have worked really hard.*). The results overall in both groups were more or less the same – but then, when given a choice as to whether to do a challenging new task, the students praised for their ability were not keen, while those praised for their effort were more prepared to go for it, and when they did, they got more enjoyment out of working on the tasks. Dweck (2008, p. 72) concludes that, 'after the difficult problems, the ability students said it wasn't fun anymore. It can't be fun when your claim to fame, your special talent, is in jeopardy.'

So, the key question for us as teachers is not *whether* to praise students, but *how* to praise them so they feel more empowered. Dweck's research clearly shows that when we praise our students for who they are or for what they have managed to produce, they are pushed towards a fixed mindset which, when faced with more challenging tasks, may lead them to feel defensive of their status – smart, talented or naturally brilliant at something. Students who are praised for effort and process, are gently led towards a growth mindset, and will be more prepared to use more effort when engaging in more challenging learning processes, and the more precise the feedback is the better, e.g. *Polly, I really like how you organised your text using linking words well.*

Dweck, C. S. (2008). *Mindset: The new psychology of success*. New York: Random House Publishing.

94 Prompt students to be proactive about their learning

> Proactive learners seize the initiative and take actions to improve their learning inside and outside of class.

In organisational psychology, proactive individuals have been shown to be much more successful in a variety of careers (e.g., Fuller & Marler, 2009). Proactive learners can engage in autonomous learning and are confident about their needs as a learner (see **86**).

A framework for encouraging a proactive approach is *self-regulation* (Zimmerman, 1990). It contains three stages in a cyclic model:

1. *Forethought*: Before a task, learners set goals, think about strategies and resources needed, and they consider their expectations of success and willingness to engage.
2. *Performance*: While on task, the learner evaluates how they are progressing, thinks about strategies to use, and seeks support if needed.
3. *Self-reflection*: After a task is completed, learners take stock of how successful they were and why. They use this knowledge to inform future tasks.

Teachers can support learners' self-regulation by enabling learners to discuss their ideas of how to approach a task. It is also important that they are aware of their own strengths and areas where they may need to seek help and where to get such help. If students are working outside of class, it can be worthwhile addressing stages 1 and 3 in class so that learners can develop their awareness and learn from each other.

In class, proactive learning can be further enhanced by giving learners options and encouraging them to express their opinions about their learning preferences.

Fuller, B. Jr. & Marler, L. E. (2009). Change driven by nature: A meta-analytic review of the proactive personality literature. *Journal of Vocational Behavior, 75*(3), 329–345.

Zimmerman, B. J. (1990). Self-regulated learning and academic achievement: An overview. *Educational Psychologist, 25*(1), 3–17.

Show students how drawing can help improve their learning

Incorporating different forms of drawing can enhance the students' learning and make it more long-lasting.

'Research suggests that visualization plays an essential role not only in developing understanding and reasoning, but more generally as a means to help learners to learn, solve problems, memorise information, and communicate ideas' (Twissell, 2014, p. 188). For example, when learners make drawings while taking information from texts, it tends to be better organised and more easily integrated into their prior knowledge. In addition, learners take a more active role in the learning process, and studies have shown that the additional effort in producing pictures or graphs has significantly positive effects on long-term memory retention and test performance (Schmeck et al., 2014). Some ideas for using visuals include:

- Engage students in summarising narrative texts; while they're doing that, they should sketch a matchstick-like cartoon strip of the story's main events on the board. Later, ask them to tell anecdotes or stories, while they sketch another matchstick cartoon strip.
- Ask students to read a factual text. On the board, show them a graph/flow chart/mind-map that summarizes its key points. Later, give them similar text to read, and tell them to create their own visual representation of the text, explaining it to a partner/small group.
- When they learn a new grammatical concept, ask a volunteer to draw on the board a visual representation that explains their understanding of the concept. Ask some others to contribute to the visual map. This may give you a good overview of their comprehension of the concept you are teaching.

Twissell, A. (2014). Visualisation in applied learning contexts: A review. *Journal of Educational Technology & Society*, 17(3), 180–191.

Schmeck, A., Mayer, R. E., Opfermann, M., Pfeiffer, V. & Leutner, D. (2014). Drawing pictures during learning from scientific text: Testing the generative drawing effect and the prognostic drawing effect. *Contemporary Educational Psychology*, 39(4), 275–286.

96 Build in brain breaks

> When concentrating for longer periods of time, the ability to concentrate decreases. Taking a brain break allows for a quick reboot for learning.

Brain breaks refer to short, regular breaks that can be built into classroom life (online or in person) to allow learners to momentarily de-stress, re-focus, and refresh so they are ready to re-engage.

Brain breaks can take different formats such as breathing exercises, physical movement, meditation, working on puzzles or other quick brain teasers. Keeping a link to the task or content of the class can make re-engagement afterwards easier. It is important when planning in a brain break to consider two aspects: (1) when to introduce this so it does not disturb concentrated work but comes at a point when students are ready for the break; and (2) that the brain break is not so disruptive that it takes a long time for the students to get back on task and re-focus.

Some examples of brain breaks for the language classroom could be:

- Working on sports, students stand up and pretend through mime to be skiing down a mountain without moving from their spot but squatting and leaning side to side.
- Working on the environment, students close their eyes and take a guided journey with the teacher using prompts to imagine a beautiful forest or tropical beach walk.
- Working on any topic, students do a quick word game or puzzle such as writing a word from the text on their partner's back and guessing what word it is.
- Students look at an inspiring picture and describe what they see and like about it.
- Doing short mindful exercises.

Weslake, A. & Christian, B. J. (2015). Brain breaks: Help or hindrance? *Teach Collection of Christian Education*, 1(1), 38–46.

For feedback to achieve its potential, learners must see the need for it, its value, and must engage with it.

Hattie and Timperley (2007, p. 81) state, 'Feedback is one of the most powerful influences on learning and achievement, but this impact can be either positive or negative.' They suggest that effective feedback covers three main points:

1. Where am I going? (The goals) – Feed Up
2. How am I going? (My current performance/level) – Feed Back
3. Where to next? (Strategies and pathways of action) – Feed Forward

Feedback can be more effective when the learner shares ownership of the process with the teacher. One way to do this is to see feedback as a dialogue. Feedback can be a two-way process with teachers providing learners feedback on their performance and approaches to learning, but learners can also provide teachers with feedback on what kind of support they find helpful or feel is missing. Such dialogue works best when an atmosphere of mutual trust and respect has been established.

The feedback dialogue can also be directed by learners (see 77). For example, learners can ask teachers for feedback on specific aspects of their work such as in a cover letter or digital dialogue box. Teachers may respond in writing or audio-recordings which can easily be embedded digitally.

Naturally, in large classes, this can be time-intense; however, teachers can maintain a dialogic element with learners sharing their comments with teachers individually, but teachers providing just one whole-class response (e.g., *Dear Class 7B, Thanks for your stories about elephants. The things I really enjoyed in the texts were ... Several of you asked me to look specifically at the use of adverbs and this is what I noticed ...*).

Hattie, J. & Timperley, H. (2007). The power of feedback. *Review of Educational Research*, 77(1), 81–112.

98 Encourage your students to keep a portfolio

> A portfolio can increase learner autonomy and create an empowering vision of students' learning for their future.

Keeping a learning portfolio can have various advantages for students. By collecting evidence of their progress, students become more actively engaged in observing their learning process, and by drawing conclusions from their observations, they develop their metacognitive knowledge about themselves and language learning as a process. Portfolios may also be used as an alternative kind of assessment that complements more formal methods of evaluation which can boost learner autonomy and motivation (Little, 2009). Portfolios have a forward-looking dimension too in that they can give future employers or teachers insights into a student's achievements at various stages – insights that go beyond what grades or certificates can convey.

An e-portfolio has clear advantages over a hard-copy one, as storing, updating and adding multimedia files to it is easier, and students can maintain data over several years. For those in low resource settings, a folder of work can work just as well.

- Show students how they could use their portfolio to collect evidence of their learning. Ask them what they could include to showcase their language learning to future teachers or employers. Help them to reflect on work they are proud of and wish to show to others, maybe including family members.
- For e-portfolios, show students how to set up a folder with sub-folders using a variety of media. The items could include videos of roleplays, show-and-tell presentations (filmed on a mobile), stories they have written, audio-recordings, etc.
- Remind them regularly to keep their portfolio up-to-date and get them to prompt each other about things to add, providing opportunities also in class to share with each other if they wish.

Little, D. (2009). Language learner autonomy and the European language portfolio: Two L2 English examples. *Language Teaching*, 42(2), 222–233.

> **Many students use inefficient study strategies; it is relatively easy to teach them to use more efficient ones.**

Most teachers inform their learners ahead of a test or an exam *what* they are supposed to be studying, but it is often up to the students *how* they prepare. Dunlosky et al. (2013) reviewed more than 700 research papers into learning strategies. Their meta-study shows that many commonly used strategies are inefficient, although students tend to be convinced of their efficacy. Inefficient strategies include (1) re-reading (students reading lists of words, texts, etc. repeatedly, but also (2) highlighting, and (3) underlining, often used in combination with re-reading. These strategies do not engage students deeply enough cognitively. Similarly, another flawed strategy is cramming – studying for hours during the day (or night) before an exam. This fails to create sustainable results because learners do not get sufficient sleep in between the learning which is necessary to cement learning in the brain (Dehaene, 2020).

However, teachers can work with learners explicitly on how to learn more effectively, discussing what learning strategies are available. Two of the most efficient learning strategies are *retrieval practice* (or *practice testing*) and *distributed practice* (spreading out the study over several days).

- Do practice tests and advise students to do the same test several times. They will notice their retrieval gets better each time they do it.
- Use a short retrieval activity at the beginning of each lesson. Ask students, e.g., to write down six words they learnt in the previous week, compare them with their partner's, create sentences with them, and share those with the whole class.

Dehaene, S. (2020). *How We Learn: The new science of education and the brain*. London: Penguin.

Dunlosky, J., Rawson, K. A., Marsh, E. J., Nathan, M. J. & Willingham D. T. (2013). Improving students' learning with effective learning techniques: promising directions from cognitive and educational psychology. *Psychological Science in the Public Interest, 14*(1), 4–48.

Embrace all learners' languages

> Embracing learners' diverse languages can empower
> them to engage fully in classroom life and to utilise their
> languages to support their learning.

For a long time, learners' L1s were seen as an obstacle to learning
the target language and something that should be banned from the
classroom. Thankfully, attitudes are changing and learners' multiple
languages are seen as a valuable resource and key part of learners'
identities.

One approach to teaching which embraces learners' linguistic resources
is *translanguaging*. This refers to diverse ways of supporting learners
in using their L1 or any other languages they know in the process of
learning and using the target language. It takes a flexible approach to
language use which recognises that languages are dynamic and often
overlap. It views all languages as assets that can be employed creatively
and constructively in written or spoken text production. Although the
focus remains on promoting use of the target language, other languages
are welcomed when they can support learner engagement and help
learners make useful connections across languages.

Perhaps a first step is to encourage positive attitudes towards
multilingualism among learners and fellow teachers by celebrating
knowledge of different languages. Some specific ideas for use in the
language classroom include:

- Creating multilingual dictionaries using the target language and
  other languages known by learners.
- Working on poems, song lyrics, stories, dialogues, etc. focusing on
  the target language but using other languages as a bridge or even
  integral part of the creative text.
- If students share a language, allow them to support each other
  linguistically when needed.

Conteh, J. (2018). Translanguaging. *ELT Journal*, 72(4), 445–447.

Teaching life skills in the language classrooms boosts learner motivation and empowers learners with valuable skills for life beyond the classroom.

Teachers of all subjects, including language teachers, have a history of integrating other core skills into their teaching. Previously, these were known as 21st century skills including critical thinking, creativity, communication, collaboration and digital literacy. More recently, these have been expanded to life skills or global skills. These terms recognise that learners need other skills to flourish in life and their communities, not just in the workplace. This broader notion of life skills incorporates competences such as ecoliteracy, wellbeing literacy and global citizenship.

Teachers can utilise three main approaches. Below are examples for wellbeing literacy, but the design principle applies to any life skill.

1. *Individual tasks*: Teachers can use single tasks focusing on a life skill. For example, learners can be introduced to the notion of 'savouring' which is taking mindful, conscious time to appreciate something positive – in the past, present or anticipated in the future. Learners could be asked to write a story of a time when they felt happy. They can revisit such positive memories to boost their positivity.
2. *Projects*: Teachers can explore bigger themes. For example, students could be assigned different global terms related to wellbeing such as *pura vida*, *hygge*, *ubuntu*, *mepak*, *ikigai*. They can be asked to research the terms and present their insights to the class.
3. *As a lens for teaching*: Teachers can simply try to find ways to regularly bring in a wellbeing perspective to their teaching. Perhaps they include breathing or yoga exercises every week or offer opportunities to discuss emotions on a regular basis.

Mercer, S., Hockly, N., Stobart, G. & Lorenzo Galés, N. (2019). *Global Skills: Creating empowered 21st century citizens*. Oxford: Oxford University Press.

Index